CAMBRIDGE PRIMARY
Mathematics

Learner's Book

3

Cherri Moseley and Janet Rees

CAMBRIDGE
UNIVERSITY PRESS

CAMBRIDGE
UNIVERSITY PRESS

University Printing House, Cambridge CB2 8BS, United Kingdom

Cambridge University Press is part of the University of Cambridge.

It furthers the University's mission by disseminating knowledge in the pursuit of education, learning and research at the highest international levels of excellence.

Information on this title: education.cambridge.org

© Cambridge University Press 2014

This publication is in copyright. Subject to statutory exception and to the provisions of relevant collective licensing agreements, no reproduction of any part may take place without the written permission of Cambridge University Press.

First published 2014
9th printing 2016

Printed in Dubai by Oriental Press

A catalogue record for this publication is available from the British Library

ISBN 978-1-107-66767-9 Paperback

Cover artwork: Bill Bolton

Cambridge University Press has no responsibility for the persistence or accuracy of URLs for external or third-party internet websites referred to in this publication, and does not guarantee that any content on such websites is, or will remain, accurate or appropriate.

....

NOTICE TO TEACHERS
It is illegal to reproduce any part of this work in material form (including photocopying and electronic storage) except under the following circumstances:
(i) where you are abiding by a licence granted to your school or institution by the Copyright Licensing Agency;
(ii) where no such licence exists, or where you wish to exceed the terms of a license, and you have gained the written permission of Cambridge University Press;
(iii) where you are allowed to reproduce without permission under the provisions of Chapter 3 of the Copyright, Designs and Patents Act 1988, which covers, for example, the reproduction of short passages within certain types of educational anthology and reproduction for the purposes of setting examination questions.

PHOTOGRAPHS
pp. 38 tswinner/Thinkstock; p. 59 Dragunov 1981 / istock / Thinkstock.

Introduction

This Learner's Book is a supplementary resource that consolidates and reinforces mathematical learning alongside the *Cambridge Primary Mathematics Teacher's Resource 3* (9781107668898). It acts as a useful consolidation tool for the learners by providing points for discussion to develop problem-solving skills and support learning through discovery and discussion. Rote learning and drill exercises are avoided.

Ideally, a session should first be taught using the appropriate *Core activity* in the *Teacher's Resource 3*, and then the *Learner's Book* page is used at the end of the session, or set as homework, as a means of formative assessment. There is a single page corresponding to each *Core activity* in the *Teacher's Resource 3* printed book. The *Core activity* that the page relates to is indicated at the bottom of the page.

Hints and tips are provided throughout to support the learners. They will appear as follows:

> Write a list of number pairs to help you

Please note that the *Learner's Book* on its own does not cover all of the Cambridge Primary mathematics curriculum framework for Stage 3. It needs to be used in conjunction with the *Teacher's Resource 3*.

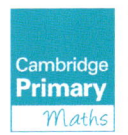

This publication is part of the *Cambridge Primary Maths project*. *Cambridge Primary Maths* is an innovative combination of curriculum and resources designed to support teachers and learners to succeed in primary mathematics through best-practice international maths teaching and a problem-solving approach.

Cambridge Primary Maths brings together the world-class Cambridge Primary mathematics curriculum from Cambridge International Examinations, high-quality publishing from Cambridge University Press and expertise in engaging online enrichment materials for the mathematics curriculum from NRICH.

Teachers have access to an online tool that maps resources and links to materials offered through the primary mathematics curriculum, NRICH and Cambridge Primary mathematics textbooks and e-books. These resources include engaging online activities, best-practice guidance and examples of *Cambridge Primary Maths* in action.

The Cambridge curriculum is dedicated to helping schools develop learners who are confident, responsible, reflective, innovative and engaged. It is designed to give learners the skills to problem solve effectively, apply mathematical knowledge and develop a holistic understanding of the subject.

The *Cambridge Primary Maths* textbooks provide best-in-class support for this problem-solving approach, based on pedagogical practice found in successful schools across the world. The engaging NRICH online resources help develop mathematical thinking and problem-solving skills. To get involved visit www.cie.org.uk/cambridgeprimarymaths

The benefits of being part of *Cambridge Primary Maths* are:
- the opportunity to explore a maths curriculum founded on the values of the University of Cambridge and best practice in schools
- access to an innovative package of online and print resources that can help bring the Cambridge Primary mathematics curriculum to life in the classroom.

This series is arranged to ensure that the curriculum is covered whilst allowing teachers to use a flexible approach. The Scheme of Work for Stage 2 has been followed, though there are a few deviations. The components are:
- Teacher's Resource 3 ISBN: 9781107668898 (printed book and CD-ROM).
- Learner's Book 3 ISBN: 9781107667679 (printed book)
- Games Book 3 ISBN: 9781107694019 (printed book and CD-ROM).

Number

Hundreds, tens and ones

Let's investigate

A set of place value cards has been used to make nine three-digit numbers. Here are seven of the numbers.

Which place value cards are missing?

How many different three-digit numbers can you make with the missing place value cards?

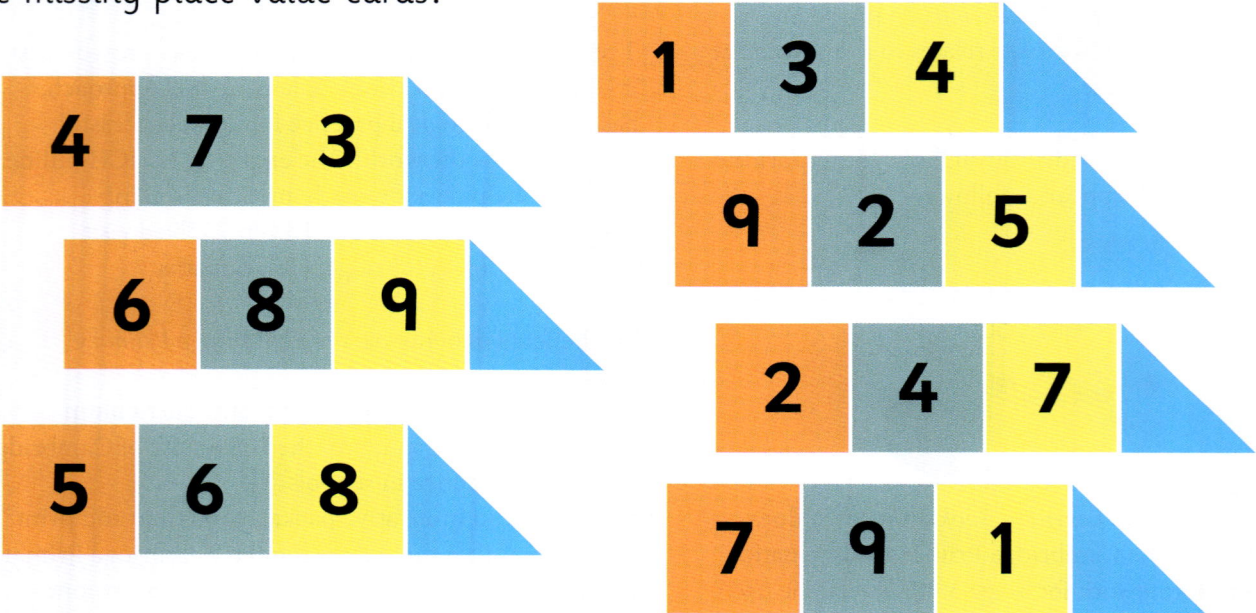

Use a set of place value cards to help you.

4 7 3

6 8 9

5 6 8

1 3 4

9 2 5

2 4 7

7 9 1

Does it matter which digit cards are the missing ones?

Will you always be able to make that many numbers? Why?

Use a set of place value cards to make nine three-digit numbers.

Show a friend seven of the numbers and challenge them to tell you the other two numbers. If the numbers are incorrect, but your friend has identified the correct cards, give them another try to guess your numbers.

Unit 1A: Core activity 1.1 Hundreds, tens and ones

1   What is the value of the 6 in each of these numbers?

   263   613   216   609

2   Write the numbers which are 10 more, 10 less, 100 more and 100 less than the numbers in Question 1.

3   The value of the digit 6 did not change in one of the numbers. Which one? Why?

4   Take the following numbers:

Hundreds	3 and 8
Tens	1 and 5
Ones	2 and 6

Use them to make as many three-digit numbers as you can.

Missing numbers

Let's investigate

The numbers have been correctly pegged on the number line below but these cards fell off.

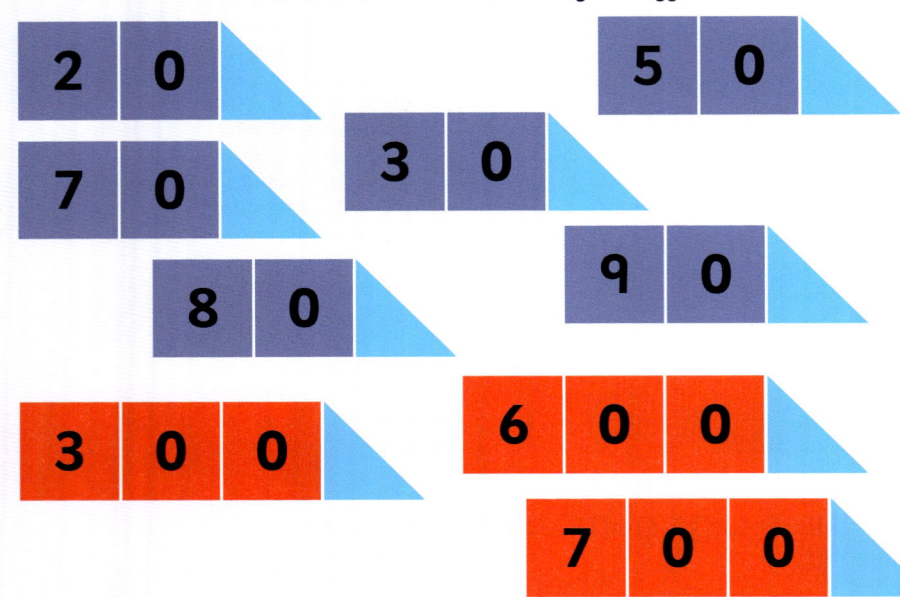

20
70
30
50
80
90
300
600
700

Sort out which card belongs with each number.

Write a list of the correct numbers and the matching missing cards.

Vocabulary

abacus: an abacus is used to show numbers and to calculate for example 421 can be shown as:

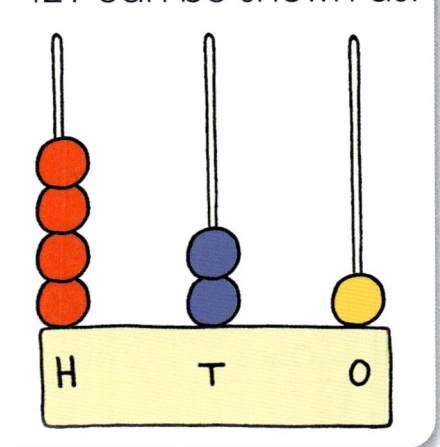

Look at where each number is pegged on the number line. What should the number be?

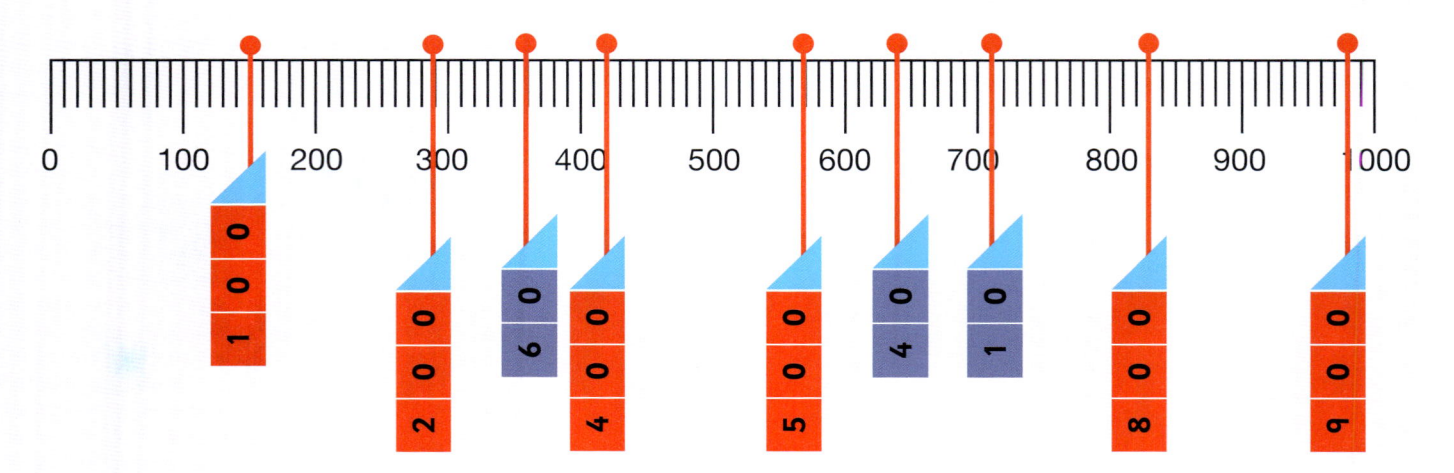

Unit 1A: Core activity 1.2 To 1000

1. The number of beads in each tower of the abacus tells you how many hundreds, tens and ones in each number.
   Write a list of the numbers shown.

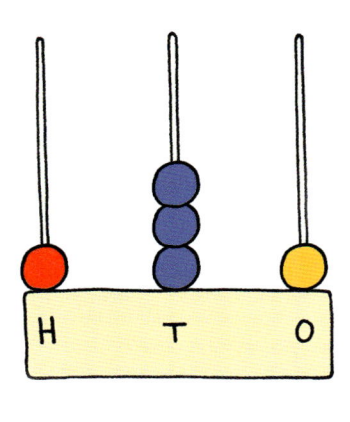

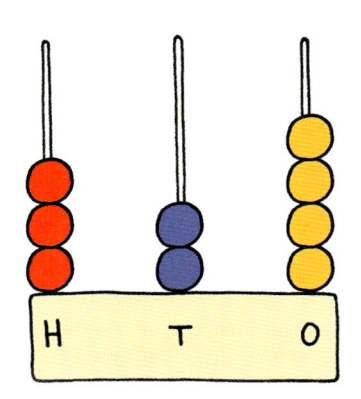

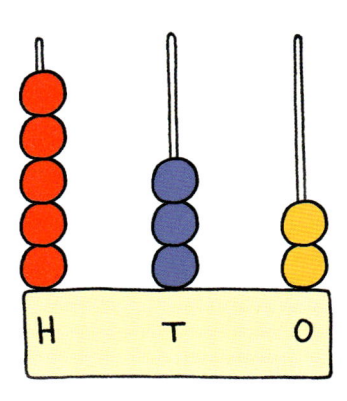

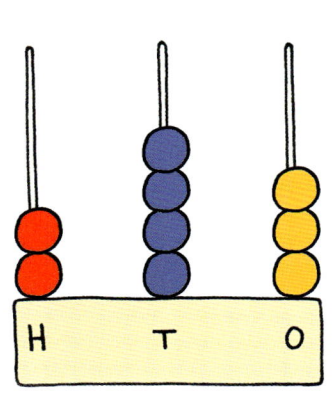

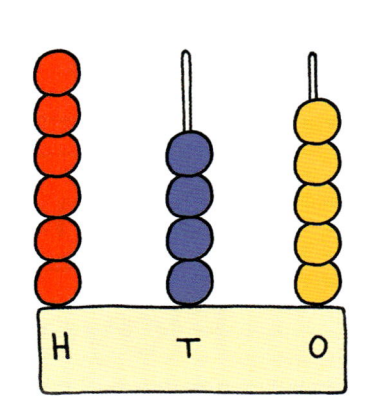

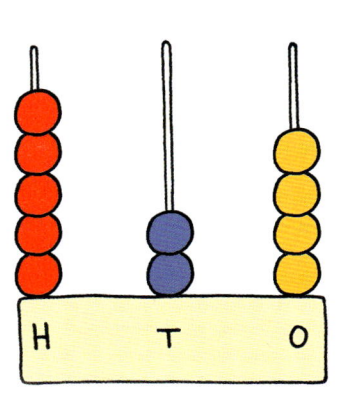

2. Put the numbers in order from the smallest to the largest.

3. Draw an abacus to show each of these numbers:

   236, 437, 352, 628, 714, 541

4. Take the place value cards and put the hundreds in one pile, the tens in another and the ones in the third pile. Shuffle each pile. Turn over the top card from each pile to make a three-digit number. Draw the abacus and write the matching number. Repeat.

   Work with a partner. Shuffle the cards again and take it in turns to read the number to your partner for them to draw.

Which game is which?

Let's investigate

Here are three unfinished HTO games. The learners were trying to make the lowest number, the highest number and the closest number to 500. But which game is which? How do you know?

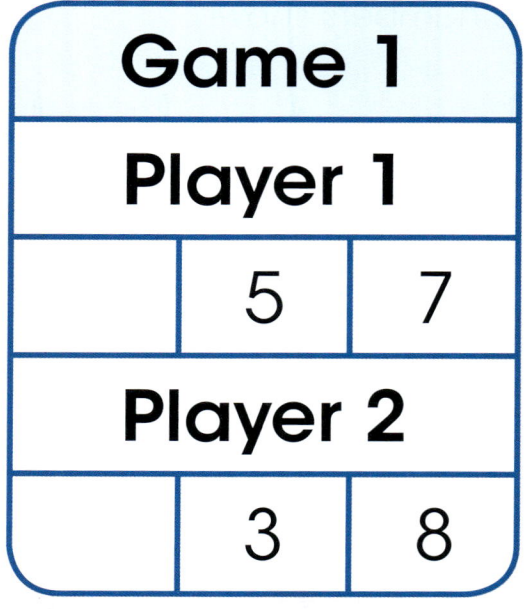

Game 1
Player 1
	5	7
Player 2
	3	8

Game 2
Player 1
4		9
Player 2
	7	2

Game 3
Player 1
	5	1
Player 2
6		2

Play a round of HTO, stopping after four digit cards have been placed. Challenge some learners to tell you which game you were playing.

> Look at where the digit cards have been placed. Where would you put each card if you were trying to make the lowest number? Or the highest number? Or the number closest to 500?

1   Here are four digits.

    | 7   4   9   1 |

    (a) Make the biggest three-digit number you can with any three of these digits
    (b) Make the smallest three-digit number you can with any three of the digits in question 1.

2   (a) What is the largest three-digit number you can make with a set of digit cards?
    (b) What is the largest three-digit number you can make with a set of hundreds, tens and ones place value cards?

3   (a) What is the smallest three-digit number you can make with a set of digit cards?
    (b) What is the smallest three-digit number you can make with a set of hundreds, tens and ones place value cards?

4   Which number needs to go in each box?
    (a) ? + 20 + 1 = 421
    (b) 100 + ? + 8 = 148
    (c) ? + 70 + 7 = 777
    (d) 800 + ? + 5 = 865

5   (a) Which is less, 4 hundreds or 44 tens? How do you know?
    (b) Which is more, 8 hundreds or 88 tens? How do you know?
    (c) Which is less, 2 tens and 3 ones or 3 tens and 2 ones? How do you know?

At the store

Let's investigate

Vocabulary

solve: find the answer.

Solve these word problems using addition or subtraction. Draw a picture or write a number sentence to show how you solved them.

Use place value cards or base ten equipment to help you.

1. The store has 21 packs of sweets left. 30 packs are delivered to the store. How many packs do they have now?

2. The store has 34 apples. 20 are sold. How many are left?

3. The baker made 248 cakes. 100 were bought for a party. How many cakes were left?

4. The store had 120 oranges. Another 100 were delivered. How many oranges does the store have now?

5. There were 84 newspapers delivered to the store this morning. 60 were sold before noon. How many were left to sell in the afternoon?

6. The store had 160 eggs but 40 had gone off. How many were left to sell?

7. The store had 107 packs of rice. 200 packs are delivered. How many packs does the store have now?

8. 140 boxes of tea were delivered to the store. There were 37 left on the shelf. How many boxes of tea does the store have now?

9. Bags of potatoes come in three different sizes 3 kg, 5 kg and 10 kg. The store has five 3 kg bags, four 5 kg bags and two 10 kg bags. How many kg of potatoes does the store have?

10. Make up a story for these number sentences.

    $175 + 20 = 195$

    $64 - 20 = 44$

    $212 + 100 = 312$

    $520 - 300 = 220$

    Tell one of your stories to a friend and listen to one of theirs. Can you both tell which number sentence was used?

Wildlife puzzle

Let's investigate

What is the value of each animal?

How many legs in this puzzle?

How did you find out?

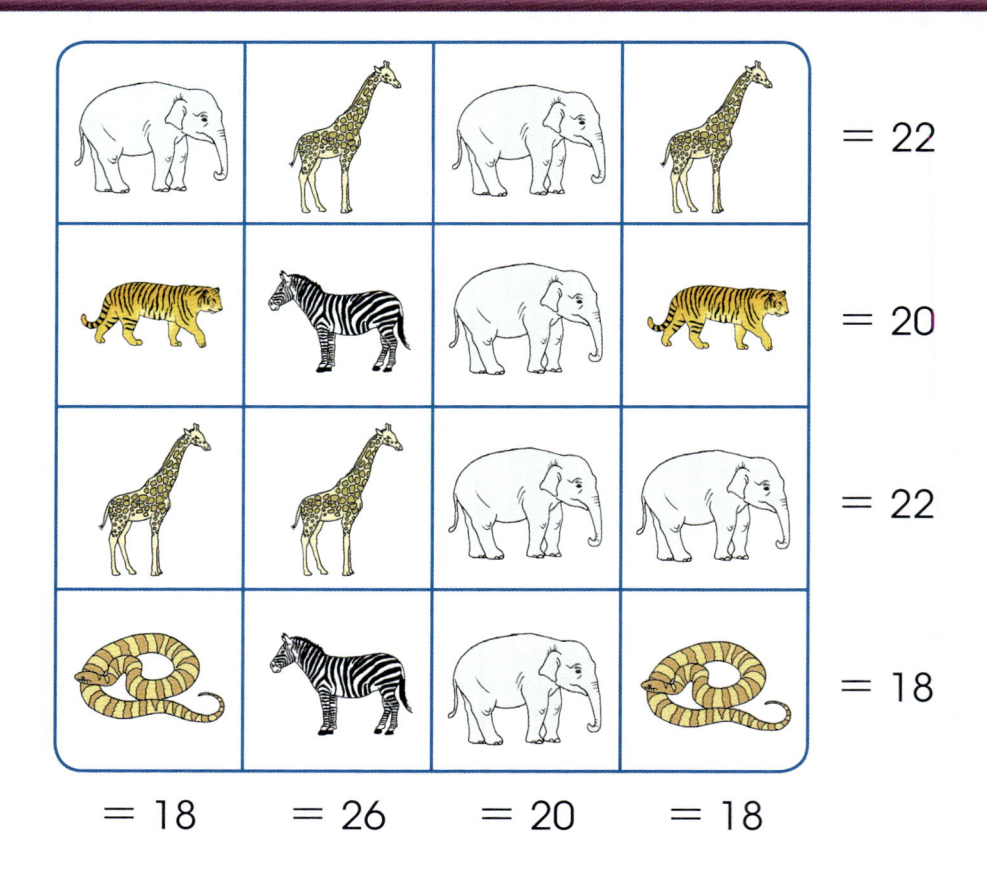

elephant	giraffe	elephant	giraffe	= 22
tiger	zebra	elephant	tiger	= 20
giraffe	giraffe	elephant	elephant	= 22
snake	zebra	elephant	snake	= 18
= 18	= 26	= 20	= 18	

Now solve these number sentences.

1 giraffe + tiger + elephant + snake + zebra = ?

2 5 giraffe = ?

3 8 tiger = ?

4 6 elephant = ?

12

Unit 1A: Core activity 3.1 Adding several small numbers

5 3 🦓 + 2 🐍 = ?

6 4 🐍 + 5 🦓 + 4 🦒 + 5 🐅 = ?

Did you notice a quick way to find the totals?

7 🦓 − 🐍 − 🐅 = ?

8 2 🦒 − 🦓 = ?

9 🦓 − 🐘 = ?

10 🦒 + 🐍 = 🐅 + ?

Make up some puzzles like this for a friend to solve.

Use pictures of something they are interested in.

Double and half

Vocabulary

inverse: the opposite of something, reversing or undoing it.

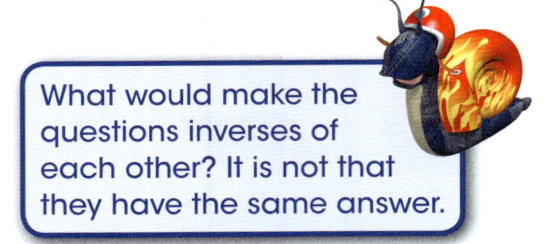

Let's investigate

Draw a grid like this one and write the answers in the matching squares.

What is half of 20?	What is double 4?	What is double 6?
What is double 14?	What is double 10?	What is half of 2?
What is half of 36?	What is half of 28?	What is double 18?
What is half of 12?	What is double 1?	What is half of 8?

What would make the questions inverses of each other? It is not that they have the same answer.

Which questions are inverses of each other?

Make up a story to go with one of these questions.

1. What is double 50?

    Write the inverse statement.

2. What is double 75?

    Write the inverse statement.

3. What is half of 50?

    Write the inverse statement.

4. What is half of 500?

    Write the inverse statement.

14

Unit 1A: Core activity 4.1 Doubling and halving

Fact family flower

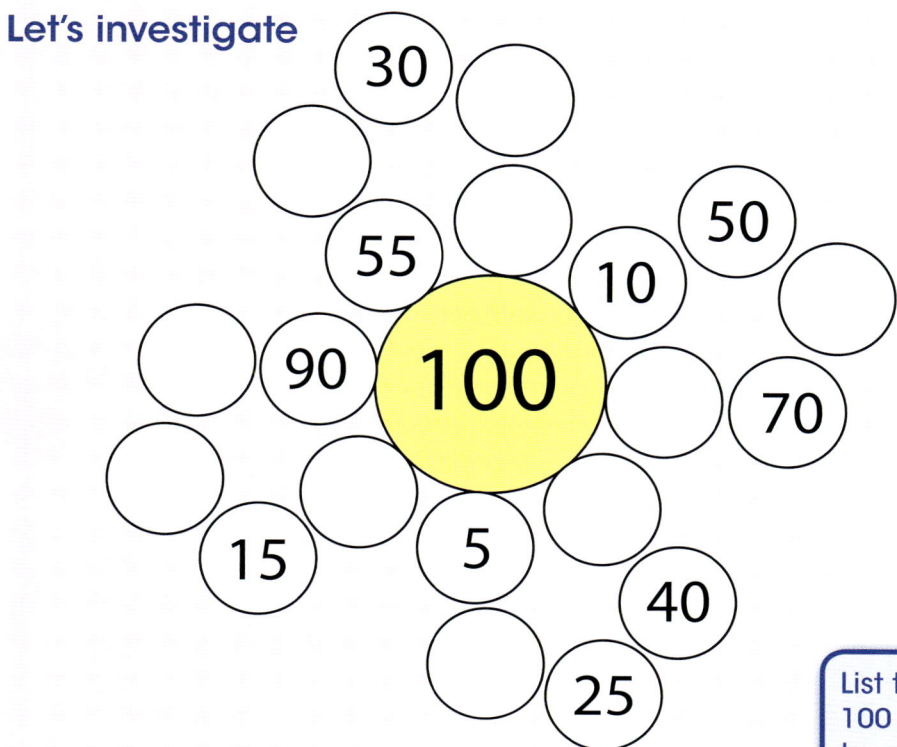

Let's investigate

Each petal has a different multiple of five on it. Which ones are missing?

Using all the numbers and zero, write the fact family for all the number pairs of multiples of five with a total of 100.

Vocabulary

multiple: when we start counting at 0 and count in steps of equal size, the numbers we say are multiples of the step size.

0, 10, 20, 30, 40, 50, 60, 70… are all multiples of 10.

List the multiples of 5 to 100 and then pair them to make 100.

1. Copy and complete:
   - (a) 5 + ? = 100
   - (b) 35 + ? = 100
   - (c) ? + 80 = 100
   - (d) ? + 15 = 100
   - (e) 100 − ? = 45
   - (f) 100 − ? = 65

2. Which number sentences would you have written if you were using number pairs for multiples of 100 with a total of 1000?

Unit 1A: Core activity 5.1 Fact families

Target 11

Let's investigate

Find the additions with a total of 11.

0 + 11	0 + 4	8 + 11	7 + 7	5 + 1	6 + 11	5 + 10	9 + 8
0 + 9	2 + 10	2 + 7	2 + 4	1 + 8	2 + 9	7 + 11	2 + 5
9 + 10	1 + 7	7 + 8	5 + 9	8 + 8	0 + 2	3 + 7	0 + 3
6 + 8	8 + 10	1 + 10		9 + 7	3 + 8	3 + 11
0 + 1	5 + 7	9 + 11	11	5 + 2	4 + 10	2 + 6
6 + 7	2 + 8	4 + 11	2 + 8	1 + 11	2 + 7	5 + 5	2 + 2
5 + 11	5 + 8	5 + 8	5 + 4	4 + 7	2 + 11	6 + 10	8 + 7
2 + 1	3 + 10	5 + 7	5 + 6	5 + 3	4 + 8	2 + 3	7 + 10

Use some squared paper. Draw a matching 8 by 8 square and write the answers in the matching squares.

1. Use the equals sign = to link pairs of calculations with a total of 11, for example: 1 + 10 = 6 + 5

2. Find three different pairs of calculations with the same total. Use the equals sign to link them.

3. Which of these calculations have a total of 11? Check by adding.

    (a) 27 − 18   (b) 65 − 54   (c) 91 − 79   (d) 38 − 27

4. Malik had four stickers and bought seven more.
   Joe had 15 stickers and gave three away.
   Do they now have the same number of stickers?'

5. I had 17 sweets but I ate six.
   My brother had 15 sweets and he ate four.
   Do we have the same number of sweets now?

6. Use a *Blank target board* to make a target board for any number up to 20. Swap with a friend. Can you both find the correct additions?

16

Unit 1A: Core activity 5.2 Calculation strips

Will you, won't you?

> Use what you know about the multiples of 2, 5 and 10 to help you. You could also use a 100 square to help you with the patterns.

1 Start at 0, count on in twos. Will you say 121? How do you know?

2 Start at 0, count on in fives. Will you say 95? How do you know?

3 Start at 0, count on in tens. Will you say 170? How do you know?

4 Start at 0, count on in fives. Will you say 83? How do you know?

5 Start at 0, count on in twos. Will you say 99? How do you know?

6 Start at 43, count back in steps of 2. Will you say 11? How do you know?

7 Start at 49, count back in steps of 5. Will you say 24? How do you know?

8 Start at 197, count back in steps of 10. Will you say 27? How do you know?

9 Start at 36, count back in steps of 5. Will you say 11? How do you know?

10 Start at 118, count back in steps of 10. Will you say 68? How do you know?

Make up some questions like these to ask a friend. Make sure you know the answer.

Assorted multiples

Answer these questions on multiples.

1. Write the first five multiples of 2, then 3, then 5 and then 10.

2. Which of these numbers are multiples of 3?

   > 10   15   20   25   30   35   40

3. Which of these numbers are multiples of 5?

   > 10   12   14   16   18   20   22

4. Copy and complete these sentences:

   The multiples of 10 always have _____ ones.

   The multiples of 2 are _____ numbers.

   The multiples of 5 always have _____ or _____ ones.

5. Which of these numbers should not be in the box?

   Multiples of 2

   12, 8, 15, 9, 18

   Multiples of 5

   10, 16, 30, 18, 20

Unit 1A: Core activity 6.2 Multiple fact families

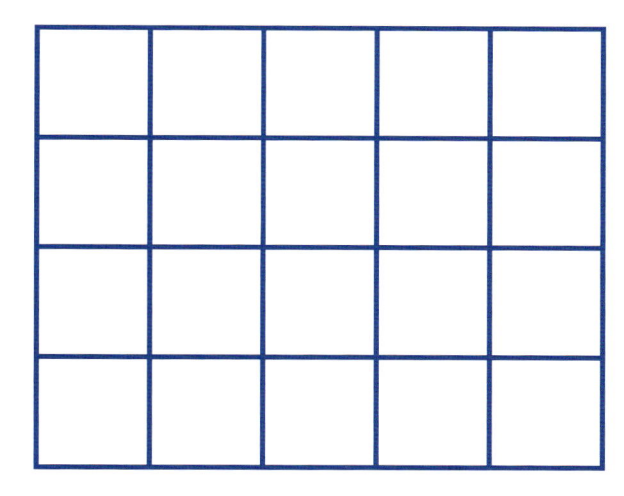

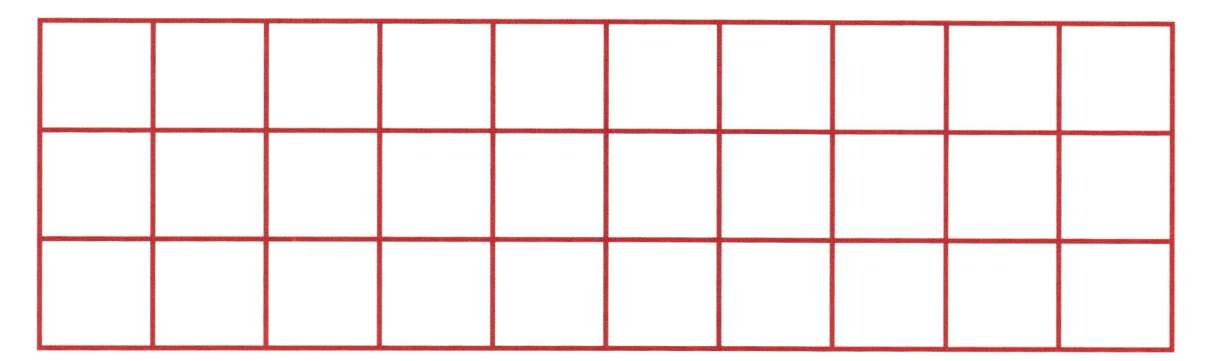

6 Write the fact family for each rectangle. Make up a number story for one of the facts in each fact family.

Write the number sentence and work out the total for each of these problems.

7 Each bag holds 10 sweets. How many sweets in seven bags?

8 Six children have new shoes. How many new shoes is that?

9 The tree is five times taller than the fence.
The fence is two metres tall. How tall is the tree?

10 Each car can carry five people. How many people could travel in seven cars?

Write some problems for a friend to solve.

Multiple multiples

Let's investigate

Ask your teacher for a copy of the *Multiples of 2, 3, 4 and 5* sheet.

Look at the key at the top of the sheet.

Choose four different colouring pencils.

Colour the top quarter of the box if the number is a multiple of 2.

Colour the bottom quarter of the box if the number is a multiple of 5.

Colour the left hand quarter if the number is a multiple of 3 and colour the right hand quarter if the number is a multiple of 4.

Colour one set of multiples at a time.

When you have finished, answer these questions.

(a) Which numbers have two colours? Why?
Write the multiplication facts for these numbers and use the equals sign to write paired facts with the same product.

(b) Which numbers have three colours? Why?
Write paired multiplication facts for four of these numbers.

(c) Which numbers have four colours? Why?
Write paired multiplication facts for each of these numbers.
Practise counting in threes and fours so that you begin to learn those times tables.

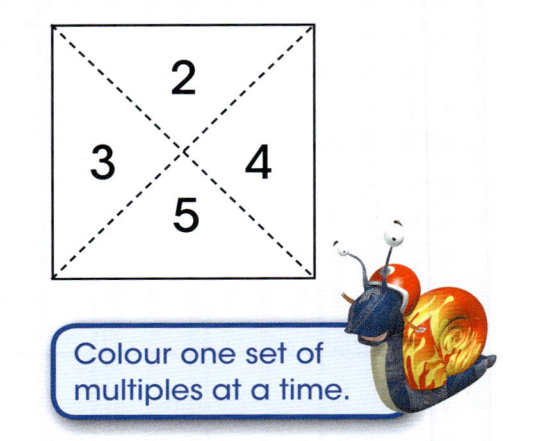

Use your 2, 3, 4 and 5 times tables to help you answer these problems:

1. There are two chocolate bars in each pack.
   - (a) How many chocolate bars in
     - (i) four packs?
     - (ii) six packs?
     - (iii) nine packs?
     - (iv) 11 packs?
   - (b) How many packs do I need to give 12 children a chocolate bar each?

2. The cake shop puts four cakes in each box.
   - (a) How many cakes in:
     - (i) two boxes?
     - (ii) five boxes?
     - (iii) seven boxes?
     - (iv) eight boxes?
   - (b) How many boxes of cakes do I need to give 24 people a cake each?

3. Some birds are standing on the top of a fence.
   - (a) If there are eight birds, how many legs are there?
   - (b) What if there were 18 legs? How many birds are there?

4. A field has horses and ducks in it.

   There are 20 legs in the field.

   How many horses? How many ducks?

   How many different possible answers can you find?

5 Sam makes gloves. He likes to count how many fingers he has made. Each glove has five fingers.

  (a) How many fingers on:
    (i) three gloves?
    (ii) seven gloves?
    (iii) 10 gloves?
  (b) On a busy morning, Sam made nine pairs of gloves. How many fingers is that?

6 There are three toy cars in a pack.

  (a) How many cars in:
    (i) two packs?   (ii) five packs?
    (iii) eight packs?   (iv) 10 packs?
  (b) I need 12 toy cars. How many packs should I buy?

7 Cookies are packed in bags of five.

  (a) How many cookies in
    (i) two bags?   (ii) five bags?
    (iii) eight bags?   (iv) nine bags?
  (b) We need 30 cookies. How many bags of cookies is that?

8 There are seven elephants resting under the trees.

  (a) How many legs?

  After a while two elephants go to the water hole for a drink.
  (b) How many elephant legs resting under the trees now?

9 There are two tigers, two elephants and four zebra drinking at a water hole.

How many legs?

10 There are nine children running races.
- (a) How many legs?

  Three children have to go home.
- (b) How many legs now?

11 Everyone needs a knife, a fork and a spoon.

That's three pieces of cutlery each.
- (a) How many pieces of cutlery are needed for
  - (i) three people?
  - (ii) six people?
  - (iii) nine people?
- (b) There are 21 pieces of cutlery to wash. How many people were there?

Geometry

2D shapes

Let's investigate

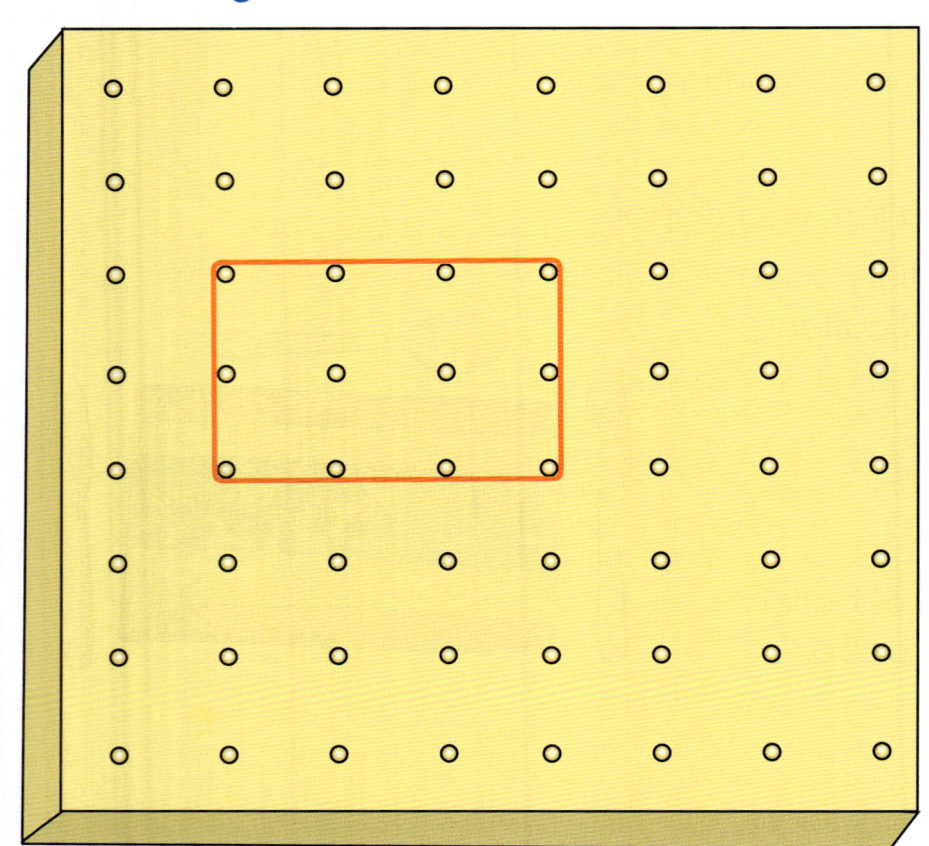

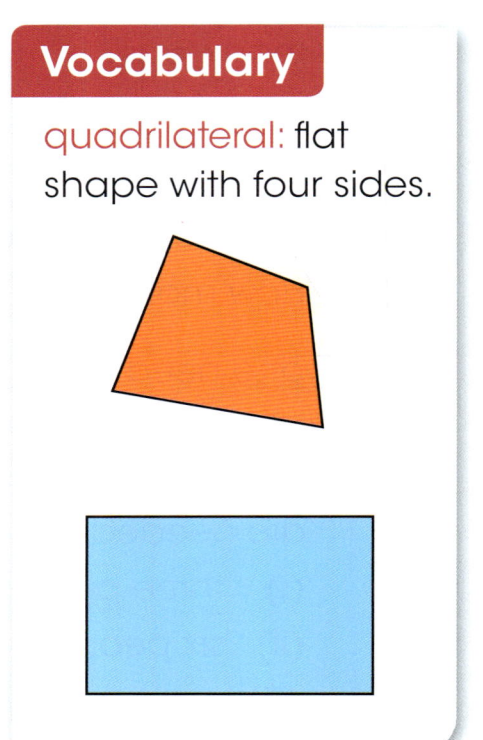

Vocabulary

quadrilateral: flat shape with four sides.

Use an 8 × 8 pinboard.

How many different quadrilaterals with right angles can you make?

How do you know when you have found them all?

1 Copy and complete this table.

Shape	Name	Sides	Corners/Vertices
rectangle			
triangle			
pentagon			
circle			
hexagon			

2 Draw and name these shapes:
   (a) I have four sides and four right angles. Both pairs of opposite sides are equal in length. One pair of sides is longer than the other.
   (b) I have six sides, not all of equal length.
   (c) I have three sides and one right angle.
   (d) I have three sides and no right angles.
   (e) I have five sides, not all of equal length.
   (f) I have four sides of equal length and four right angles.
   (g) I have six sides of equal length and no right angles.

Exploring 3D shapes

Let's investigate

Which of these nets will fold to make a cube?

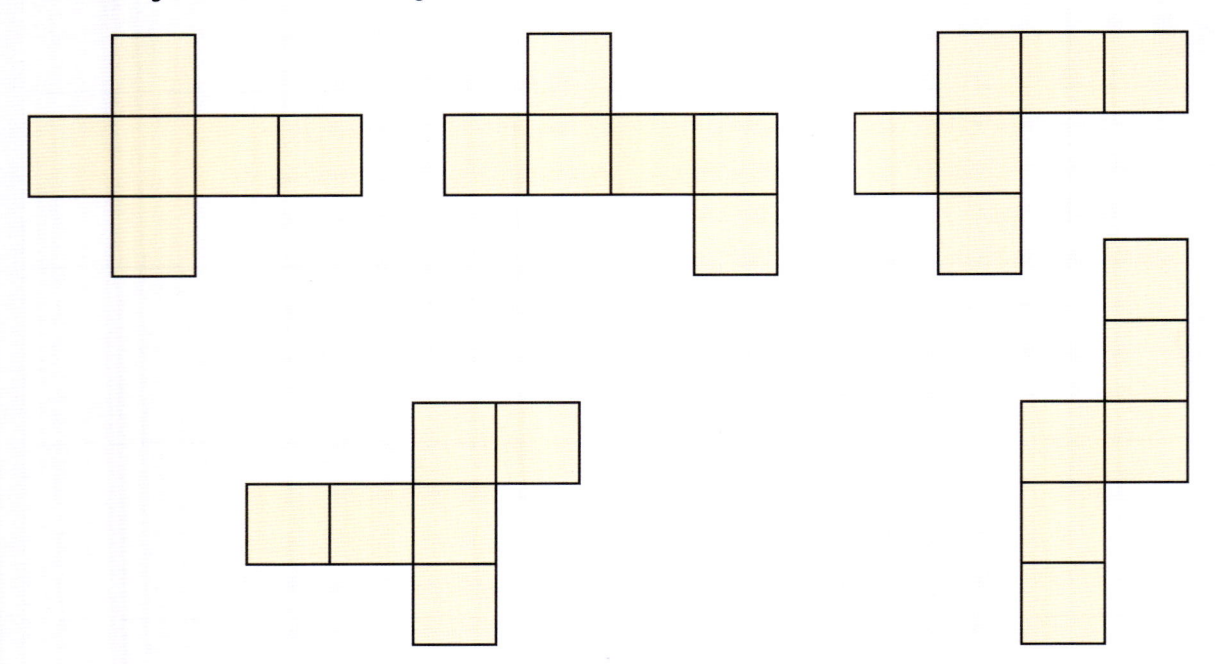

Make each one and check.

Find other nets of a cube and draw them on squared paper.

1. Draw and name the 3D shape.
   - (a) I have six faces and eight vertices.
     I have 12 edges and my faces are all the same shape.
     What am I?
   - (b) I have six faces and eight vertices.
     I have 12 edges. Four of my faces are rectangles, the other two are squares.
     What am I?
   - (c) I have three faces and 0 vertices. I have two edges.
     Two of my faces are the same, one is curved.
     What am I?

(d) I have five faces and six vertices. I have nine edges.
If you cut me in half, my end face will remain the same.
Two of my faces are triangles. The other three are rectangles.
What am I?

(e) I have one smooth surface and 0 vertices. I have 0 edges.
What am I?

(f) I have two faces. I have one vertex. I have one edge.
What am I?

2 Look at the properties of 3D shapes. Copy and complete the table.

Name of shape	Number of straight edges	Number of curved edges	Number of corners	Does it roll?	Does it stack?
Cube					
Cuboid					
Sphere					
Cylinder					
Triangular pyramid					

What do your results tell you about the shapes?

More 3D shapes

Let's investigate

Construct six square based pyramids.

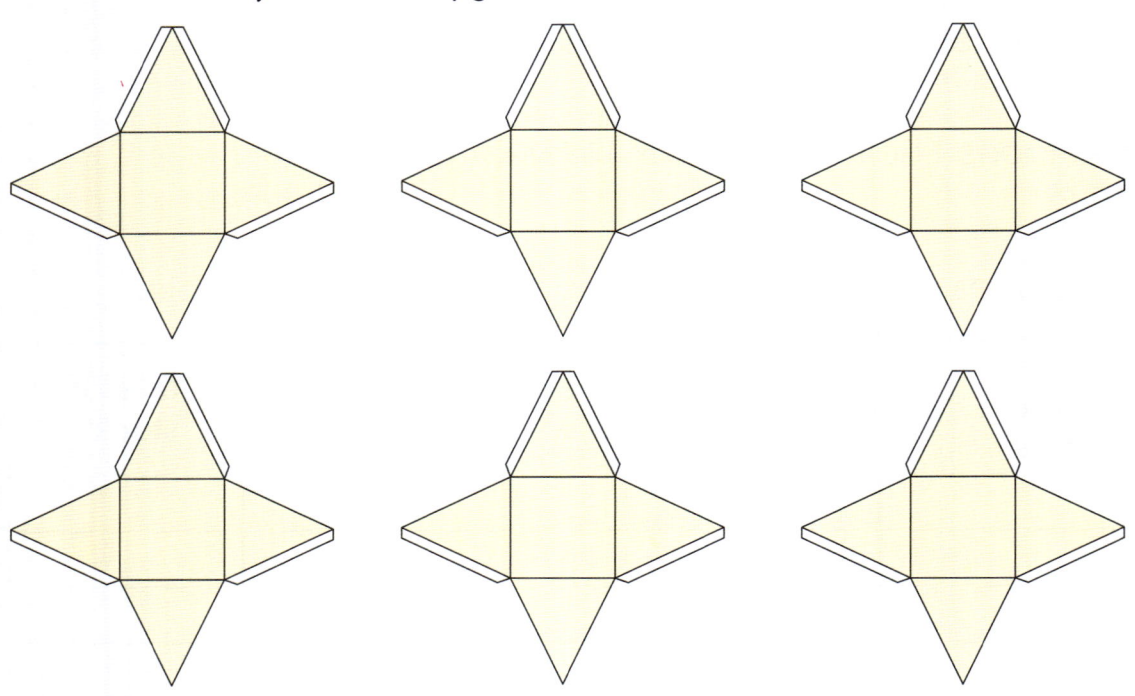

Fit them together to make a cube.

1. For each shape, write whether it is a prism or a pyramid.

   (a)   (b) 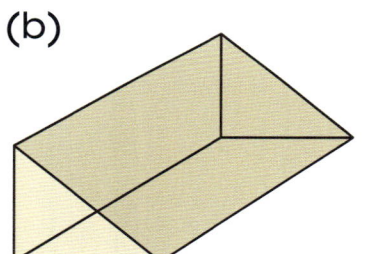   (c)

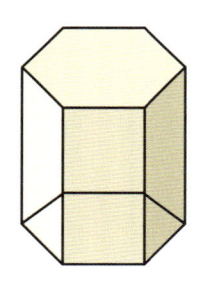

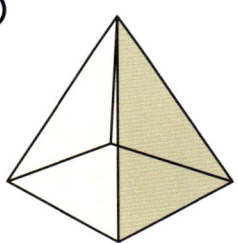

   (d) 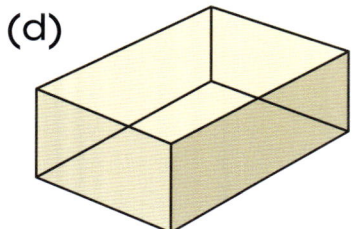   (e) 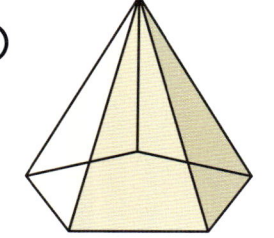   (f)

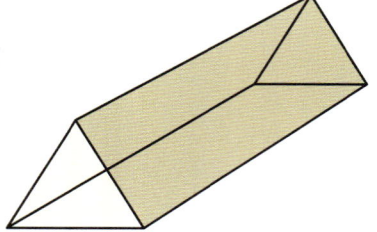

2   Copy and complete the table.

	How many … ?				
Shape name	Shape picture	Triangular faces	Rectangular faces	Edges	Corners
Cube					
Cuboid					
Triangular prism					
Square based pyramid					

3   Make these shapes using four cubes.

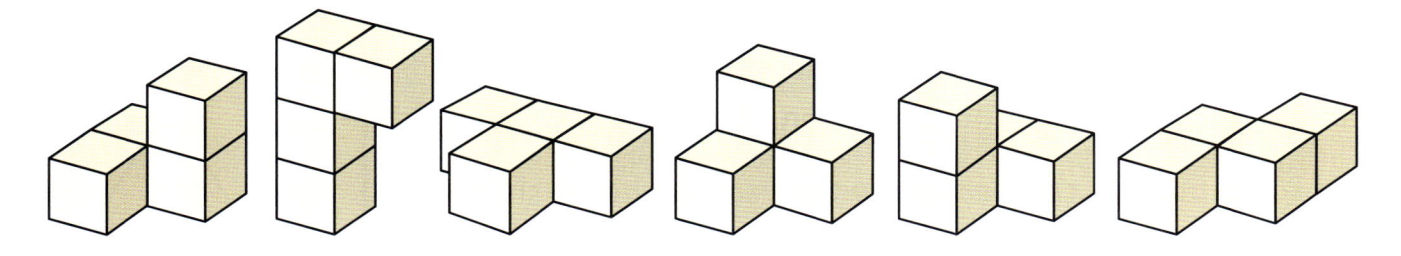

Choose one and write instructions of how to make it for someone else to follow.

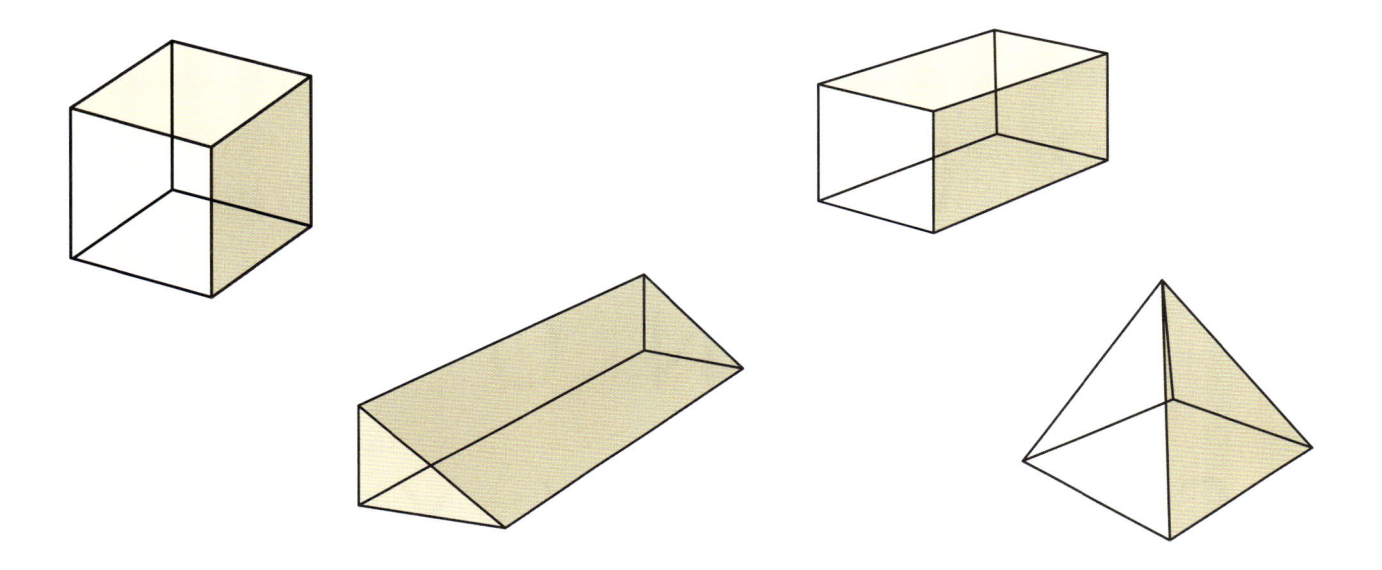

Symmetry

Let's investigate

Fold a strip of paper to make a fan.

Keep the paper fully folded.

Draw a shape on the top rectangle.

Try an outline of a person or a tree.

Make sure that your design touches both edges of the rectangle, where the folds are.

With the paper still folded, cut out the shape.

Then unfold the paper.

The first shape in the string is the same as the third, is the same as the fifth, seventh, and so on.

The same pattern can be seen with even numbered shapes.

Why does this happen?

1 Line symmetry in the alphabet. Copy these letters and mark the lines of symmetry.

A B C D E F G H I
J K L M N O P Q R
S T U V W X Y Z

2. Now answer these questions.
   (a) Which of these letters have one line of symmetry?
   (b) Which of these letters have two lines of symmetry?
   (c) Which of these letters have more than two lines of symmetry?
   (d) Which of these letters have no lines of symmetry?
   (e) How many different words can you make using letters with only one line of symmetry?
   (f) Can you make any words with the letters with only two lines of symmetry?

3. Here is half a shape and its line of symmetry. Copy the diagrams and complete the shapes.
   (a)   (b) 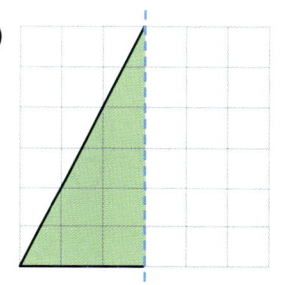   (c)

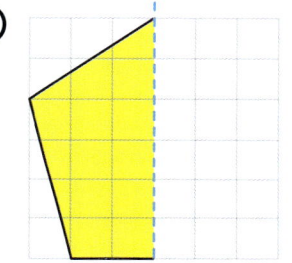

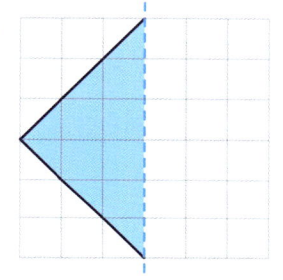

4. Copy the diagram and reflect the shape in the mirror line.

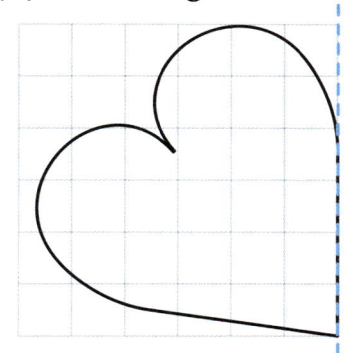

5. Fold squared paper in half, horizontally, vertically or diagonally.

   Use the fold line as the line of symmetry.

   Shade squares to make a symmetrical pattern with one line of symmetry.

   Do the same again with two folds that will give two lines of symmetry.

Routes

Let's investigate

A town wants to build a road so that these houses are divided into two groups of eight.

How many different routes can you find for the road? Note that the route does not have to be a straight line.

The hippo wants to get to the river. Each block is one step.

He always walks along the paths and always walks towards the river.

1   How many steps east can he walk before he has to turn?

2   How many step south does he have to walk in total?

3   How many steps east does he have to walk in total?

4   How many different routes can he take?

5   Can he ever walk north?

6   Can he ever walk west?

Find a way to record the different routes.

Investigate what happens if you use smaller or bigger grids.

Measure

Money

Let's investigate

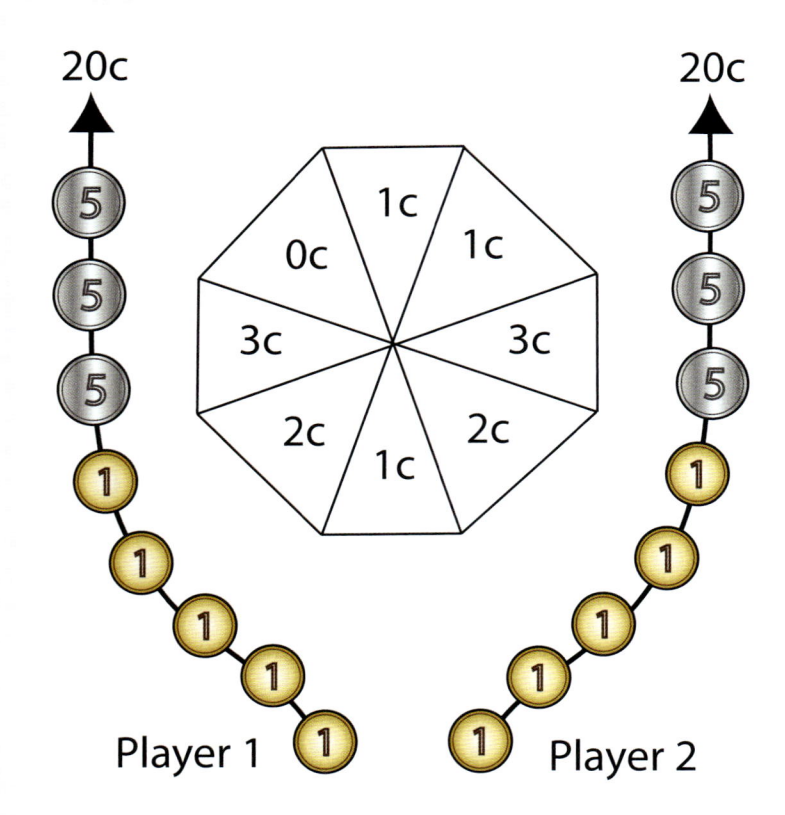

Vocabulary

cent: a coin equal to one hundredth of a dollar.

Play this game with your friend.

You will need some 1c and 5c coins and a paper clip.

Spin the paper clip on the spinner. Hold it in place with your pencil.

Collect what the clip is pointing to and put it on your board.

When you have five 1c coins, change them for a 5c coin.

The player who is the first to have 15c is the winner.

1   Look at the game board on the previous page.
   (a) How much will you have if you covered one 5 cent coin and three 1 cent coins?
   (b) If you covered all of the coins on your side of the board, how much would there be?
   (c) How many different ways can you make 10 cents?

2   Cinema tickets cost $3.45 each.
   (a) Susie buys four tickets. How much does she pay?
   (b) Josh buys a box of popcorn and two milkshakes.

   $1.85 $1.25

   How much does Josh spend altogether?

3 (a) Using coins of the same value each time, how many different ways can you make 15 cents?
   (b) How many different ways can you make 50 cents using 1 cent and 5 cent coins?

Time

1. Groups of campers were going to an island. On the first day ten went over and two came back. On the second day, twelve went over and three came back. If this pattern continues, how many would be on the island at the end of a week? How many would have left?

2. Plan a day out to last 10 hours from beginning to end. You can do more than one thing in a day.

   Use the information below.

   How many different days can you plan?

   Show the times that you leave and arrive home on both analogue and digital clocks for each day out.

Home to the bus station	30 minutes	Home to the shops	40 minutes by bike
Home to the railway station	1 hour	Shopping	2 hours
Walk from the railway station to the beach	15 minutes	Swim in the pool	1 hour
Train to the beach	15 minutes	Stay at the funfair	4 hours
Ride your bike to the funfair	20 minutes	Play on the beach	2 hours
Bus to the swimming pool	10 minutes	Drinks anywhere	10 minutes
Home to the shops	20 minutes by car	Meal anywhere	30 minutes

Unit 1C: Core activity 10.1 Clock times

3 (a) Write down the time shown on each of these clocks.

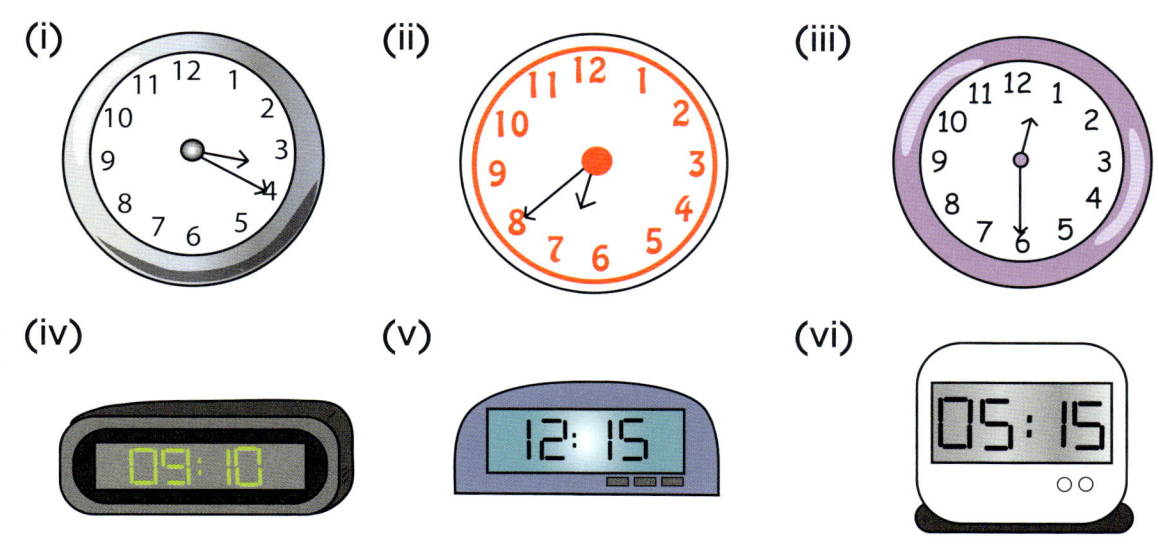

(i) (ii) (iii)

(iv) 09:10   (v) 12:15   (vi) 05:15

(b) For each clock, draw clocks to show the time 10 minutes before and five minutes after the time shown. (You will need a copy of the *Blank clocks* photocopy master from your teacher.)

Time and growth

Let's investigate

Sharks can continuously regrow teeth throughout their lifetime. As one row of teeth wears out, the next row moves forward to replace them.

If there are 38 teeth in a row and the front row of teeth are replaced every week in a growing shark, how many teeth will a shark lose in one month?

In March Joe planted a pepper seed in a pot in his shed.

At the beginning of June he put the pepper plant in its pot in the garden.

On the same day he planted a bean in a different pot.

Ten days later the bean plant was 1 cm tall.

Joe measured his pepper plant and it was 38 cm tall.

Every morning Joe measured his two plants.

On the morning of the next day the bean plant had grown another 2 cm

Each day it had grown double the amount it had grown the day before.

The pepper plant grew 5 cm every day.

1. What height was the bean plant when Joe started measuring (Day 1)?
2. How tall was it the next day (Day 2)?
3. What height was the pepper plant when Joe started measuring?
4. How tall was the bean plant on Day 4?
5. On which day will the two plants be the same height?
6. How tall were they then?

The orchard

Fruit trees are grown in a variety of shapes mainly to encourage more fruit to grow.

The shape of fruit trees can be changed by cutting (or 'pruning').

A **pyramid** shape allows trees to be planted closer together.

A **standard** shape helps sunlight get to the fruit so that more is produced.

The bush is easier for picking the fruit.

Use the table to find the answers to the questions.

Apples and pears	Yield per year		Spacing	
	Apples	Pears	In rows	Rows apart
Bush	25–50 kg	20–45 kg	4–5 m	4–5 m
Pyramid	5–7 kg	3–5 kg	1.5–2 m	2 m
Standard	50–200 kg	40–100 kg	6–10 m	6–10 m

The orchard is 20 m wide and 30 m long.

1. How many (a) bush trees (b) pyramid trees (c) standard trees could be planted?

2. What is the **heaviest** weight of apples per year that you could expect if all the trees are:

    (a) bush trees   (b) pyramid trees   (c) standard trees?

3. What is the **lightest** weight of pears per year that you could expect if all the trees are:

    (a) bush trees   (b) pyramid trees   (c) standard trees?

4. (a) If the orchard was twice as long would you get twice the weight of fruit?
    (b) If the orchard was twice as wide would you get twice the weight of fruit?
    (c) If the orchard was twice as long and twice as wide how many times more weight of fruit?

5. Which tree would you choose? Why?

How much fruit?

Let's investigate

You've just bought 10 trees.

You want to plant them in five straight lines with four trees in each line.

How are you going to do it?

1. Farmer Joe kept records of his fruit trees over four years.

   This is what he found.

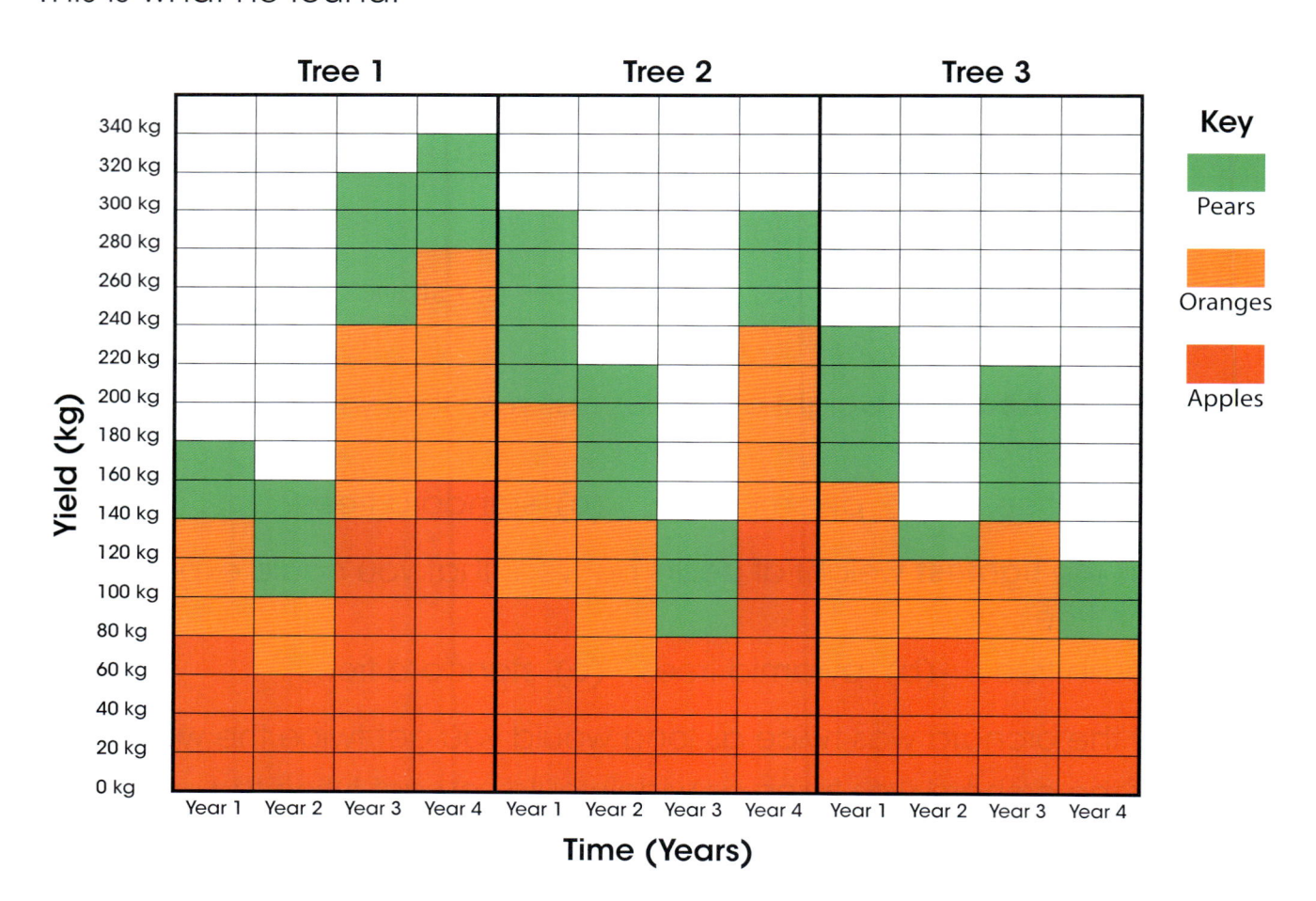

(a) Which tree gave the most fruit in the first year?
(b) Which tree gave the most fruit in the third year?
(c) Which tree gave the most fruit over four years?
(d) Which tree gave the least fruit over four years?
(e) Which two trees should Farmer Joe keep and which tree should he get rid of?

Explain why.

2 Farmer Joe collected all of the fruit ready to be sold in the shop.

Look at the scales.
(a) How much does each lot of fruit weigh in kilos and grams?

Bag A

Bag B

(b) How much does each bag weigh in grams?

Bag C

Bag D

(c) Round the weight of each bag to the nearest kilogram.

Bag E

Bag F

3   Farmer Joe plants some young fruit trees.

Write the heights of each tree in (a) metres (b) cm (c) mm.

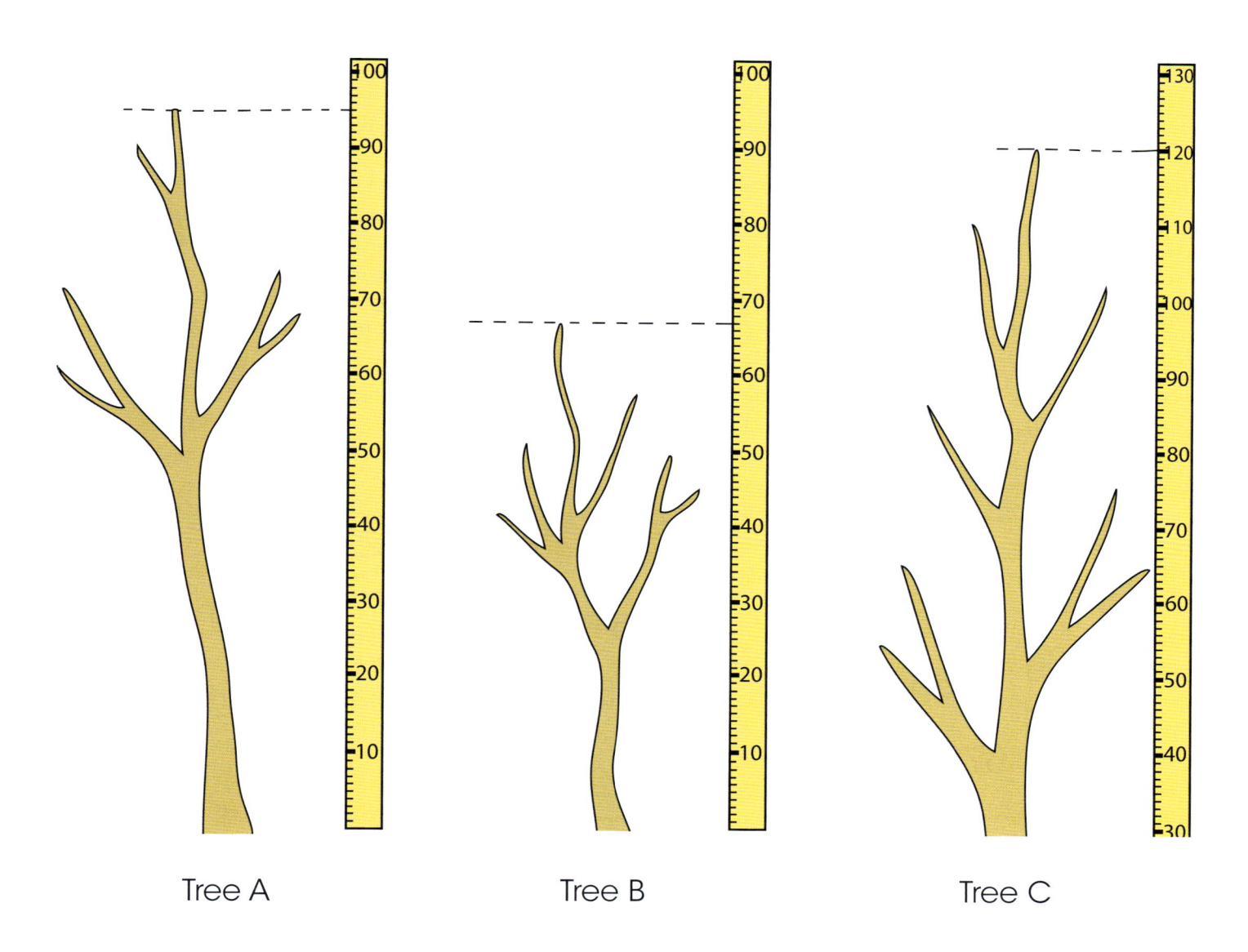

Tree A

Tree B

Tree C

43

Number

Number jars

Let's investigate

How many different three-digit numbers can you make from these digits?

Write them in order, starting with the smallest.

2 4 5 7 8

Use place value cards to help you.

Put the numbers in each jar in order. Start with the smallest.

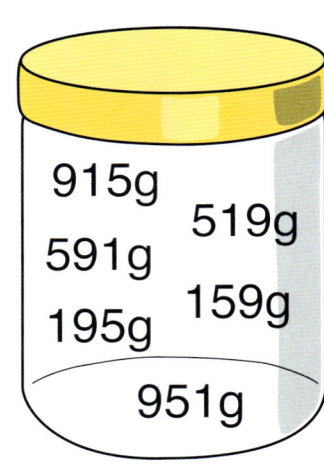

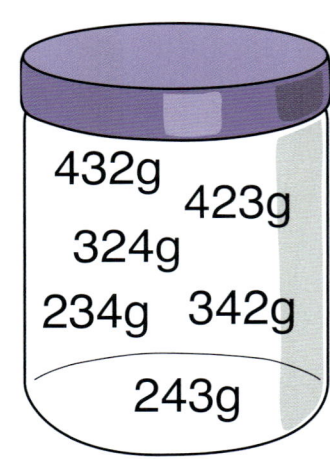

Jar 1: 876g, 867g, 768g, 786g, 687g, 678g

Jar 2: 915g, 519g, 591g, 159g, 195g, 951g

Jar 3: 432g, 423g, 324g, 234g, 342g, 243g

Put the numbers in each jar in order. Start with the largest.

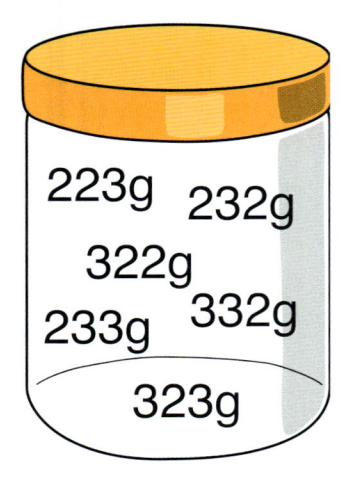

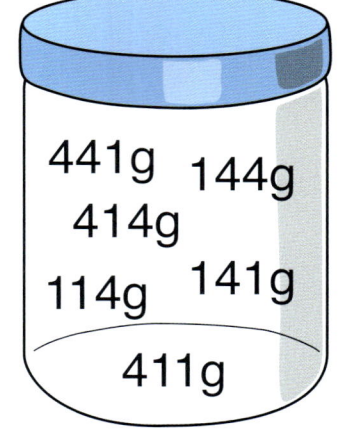

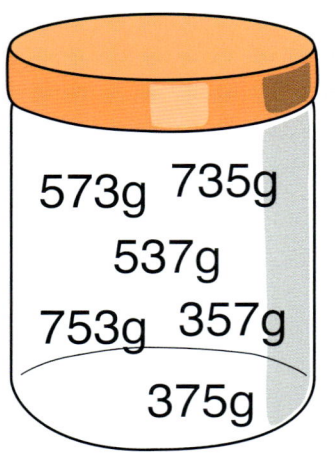

Jar 4: 223g, 232g, 322g, 233g, 332g, 323g

Jar 5: 441g, 144g, 414g, 114g, 141g, 411g

Jar 6: 573g, 735g, 537g, 753g, 357g, 375g

44

Unit 2A: Core activity 12.1 Three-digit numbers

Comparing measures

Let's investigate

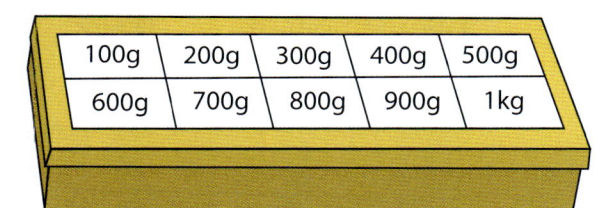

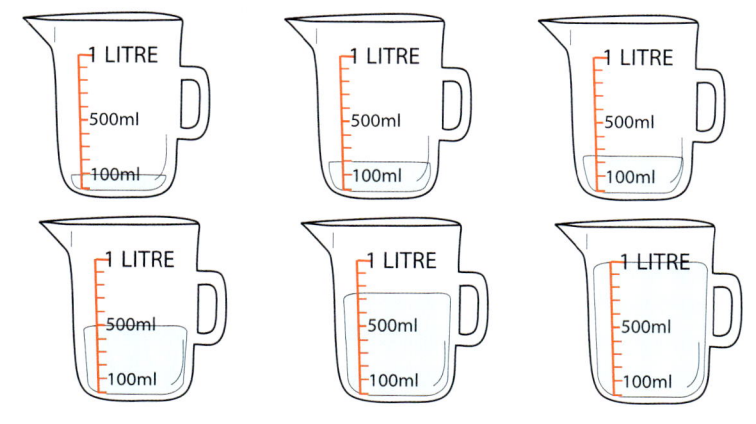

100g	200g	300g	400g	500g
600g	700g	800g	900g	1kg

Vocabulary

inequality: not equal. A number sentence using < and > but not =.

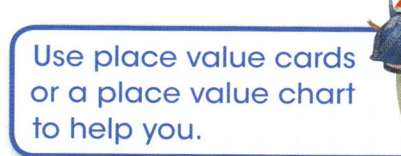

Use place value cards or a place value chart to help you.

$100\,g + 300\,g < 500\,g$ $750\,ml > 500\,ml + 100\,ml$

Write some inequalities using these weights or capacities.
Use add + and subtract − as well as less than < and greater than >.

Swap inequalities with a friend and check each others.

1. Copy and complete. Write < or > between the numbers to make the inequality true.
   - (a) 400 ? 200
   - (b) 300 ? 100
   - (c) 300 ? 400
   - (d) 250 ? 750
   - (e) 600 ? 700
   - (f) 600 ? 200

2. Copy and complete. Write a number in the box to make the inequality true.
   - (a) 30 < ? < 50
   - (b) 70 < ? < 100
   - (c) 100 > ? > 50
   - (d) 300 < ? < 350
   - (e) 100 > ? > 80
   - (f) 200 > ? > 100

Unit 2A: Core activity 12.2 Comparing numbers

45

Question time

Answer these questions. Show how you reached your answer.

Remember the effect of multiplying numbers by 10.

1   Pencils come in packs of 10. The shop has 38 packs.

    How many pencils do they have?

2   10 children can sit at a table.

    How many tables are needed for 170 to sit down?

3   Each team has 10 players. There are 39 teams in the tournament.

    How many players altogether?

4   The recipe for one serving of soup needs 30 g of potato. I need to make enough for 10 people.

    How much potato do I need?

5   A pipe is 78 cm long.

    How long will 10 pipes be? Write the length in metres.

6   A spoon hold 10 ml of syrup. I put 13 spoonfuls in my cake.

    How much syrup did I add?

7   There are 18 bananas in each bunch.

    How many in 10 bunches?

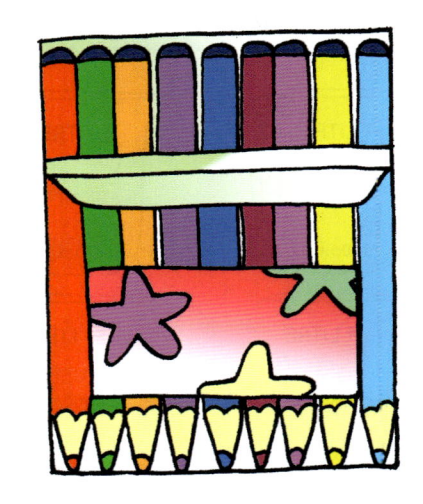

8 A bucket holds 10 litres of water. It takes 37 buckets to fill the bath.

How many litres in the bath?

9 There are 48 apples in a box. A shopkeeper buys 10 boxes.

How many apples does he buy?

10 We need 500 kg of sand. Sand comes in 50 kg bags.

How many bags will we need?

11 A fence is 76 cm tall.

How tall would it be if it was 10 times higher? Write the height in metres.

12 My carrot cake recipe needs 90 g of carrot.

I want to make a cake 10 times bigger.

What weight of carrots will I need?

Make up a question for a friend to answer using cm, m, g, kg, ml or l.

Your question might ask them to multiply something by 10 or ask how many tens are needed to make a particular amount.

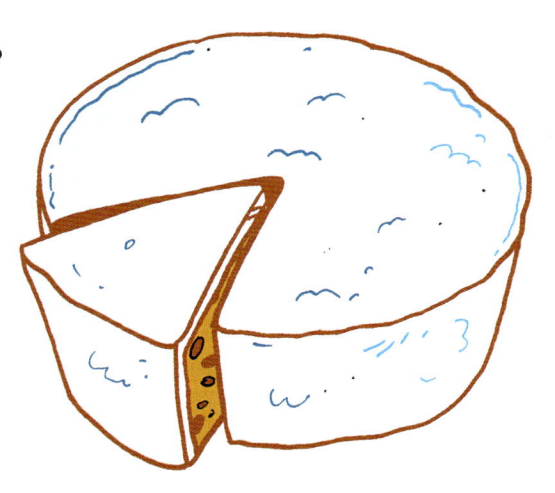

Rounding to the nearest 10 and 100

Let's investigate

(a) Round these numbers to the nearest 10.

23	335	43	29	45
178	87	646	113	65
92	169	39	425	72
216	31	184	34	317
48	558	237	361	198

Hint: Use some squared paper to help you draw some 5 by 5 grids to record your answers in.

Check what happens to numbers around 440 to 500 when rounded to the nearest 1000.

(b) Now round your new numbers to the nearest 100.

(c) Return to the original set of numbers above. Round them to the nearest 100.

(d) Compare the two sets of numbers. Are they the same? Which numbers are different? Why?

(e) What does this tell you about rounding?

Challenge: Which numbers would be incorrect if you rounded to the nearest 10, then 100, then 1000, rather than rounding straight to the nearest 1000?

1. Round each amount to the nearest 10c.
   - (a) $1.23
   - (b) $2.47
   - (c) 67c
   - (d) 36c
   - (e) 97c
   - (f) 12c

   Which amounts have been rounded down? If these were prices in a shop, would the shopkeeper accept the rounded down amount?

2. Round each length to the nearest 100 cm.
   - (a) 78 cm
   - (b) 145 cm
   - (c) 234 cm
   - (d) 319 cm
   - (e) 187 cm
   - (f) 264 cm

   Which amounts did you round up?

3. Round each weight to the nearest 10 g
   - (a) 37 g
   - (b) 49 g
   - (c) 21 g
   - (d) 75 g
   - (e) 84 g
   - (f) 56 g

   Which amounts did you round down?

4. Round each number to the nearest 10.
   - (a) 84
   - (b) 121
   - (c) 68
   - (d) 240
   - (e) 43
   - (f) 103

5. Round each amount to the nearest 100 ml
   - (a) 45 ml
   - (b) 82 ml
   - (c) 175 ml
   - (d) 121 ml
   - (e) 193 ml
   - (f) 64 ml

   The total of the rounded amounts is 700 ml. Is this more or less than the total of the amounts before they were rounded? How could you find out?

Marble estimates

Vocabulary

range: the spread of numbers concerned, for example, 30 to 50.

1   A large jar holds 500 marbles when it is full.

Use what you know about fractions to help you. If a full jar holds 500 marbles, then a half full jar should hold about 250.

Estimate how many marbles in each jar.

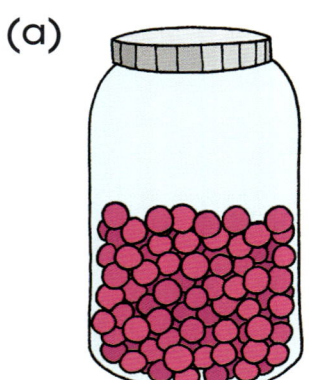

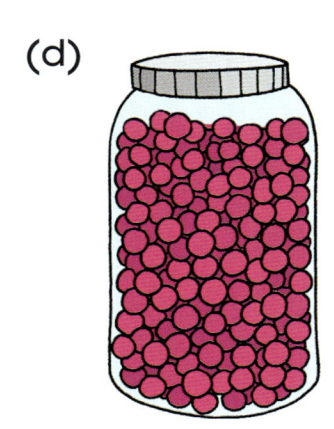

(a)   (b)   (c)

(d)   (e)   (f)

50

Unit 2A: Core activity 13.2 Estimating

2. Now estimate the total length of the lines that make up each letter to the nearest centimetre, then measure them. How close were you?

(a) W

(b) X

(c) E

(d) H

3. Draw some letters with straight lines (W, E, T, Y, A, F, H, K, L, Z, X, V, N and M are all suitable) for a friend to estimate. Alternatively, draw some for yourself using a straight edge but not a ruler. Estimate then measure them. Give yourself a point if you were within 1 cm of the measured length.

What number am I?

Solve these number puzzles.

1. Half of me is five and double me is 20.

   What number am I?

2. Half of me is two and double me is eight.

   What number am I?

3. Double me is 100, half of me is 25.

   What number am I?

4. Half of me is one and double me is four.

   What number am I?

5. Double me is 32, half of me is eight.

   What number am I?

6. Half of me is 20 and double me is 80.

   What number am I?

7. Double me is 28, half of me is seven.

   What number am I?

8. Half of me is 15 and double me is 60.

   What number am I?

9. Double me is 36, half of me is nine.

   What number am I?

Undo the doubling or halving.

10 Double me is 16, half of me is four.

What number am I?

11 Sarah has 16 marbles.

She gives half to Tom.

How many does Sarah have left?

12 I had 18 stickers on Monday.

By Friday, I had double.

How many stickers did I have on Friday?

13 I had $14 and spent half of it.

How much have I got left?

14 We followed a recipe to make eight cakes but made double.

How many cakes did we make?

15 There were 24 people at the party.

Half went home.

How many people are still at the party?

16 There were 25 people swimming.

In one hour, the number of swimmers doubled.

How many people were swimming?

17 I doubled a number and got 14.

What was my number?

18 I halved a number and got nine.

What was my number?

19 I doubled a number and got 30.

What was my number?

20 I halved a number and got one.

What was my number?

Now answer these questions.

21 How is doubling and halving the same as addition and subtraction?

22 What happens to the numbers when you double a multiple of five?

23 When have you heard the word half?

- Half each
- Half time
- ????

24 When have you heard the word double?

- Double trouble
- Seeing double
- ????

Addition walls

Let's investigate

Here is an addition wall.

The two bricks next to each other are added to find the number up above.

Here is a larger wall.

Your teacher will give you the *Addition walls* sheet.

Using the numbers 5, 6, 7, 8 and 9 in the bottom row, what is the largest total you can make on the top brick? What is the smallest?

Can you make all the numbers between the highest and lowest numbers?

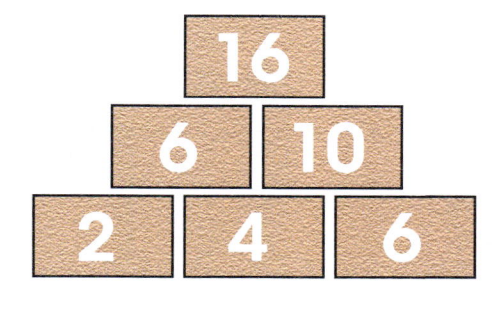

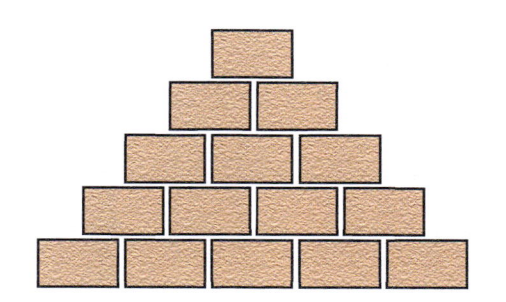

1. 68 people went into a shop on Monday and 27 on Tuesday.

    How many people went into the shop on those two days?

2. 37 white cars and 29 silver ones were sold.

    How many cars were sold altogether?

3. There are 13 girls and 15 boys in Class 1.

    How many children altogether?

Unit 2A: Core activity 15.1 Investigating addition

55

4 Class 2 has 18 boys and 17 girls.

How many children in this class?

5 (a) How many boys in Classes 1 and 2?
(b) How many girls in Classes 1 and 2?
(c) How many children altogether in Classes 1 and 2?

6 A bus picked up 28 people at the first stop and 29 at the second stop.

No one got off at the second stop.

How many people were on the bus?

7 I have some hens.

They laid 47 eggs this week and 35 eggs last week.

How many eggs altogether?

8 Add 27 to each number in the grid. Draw a 3 by 3 grid to record your answers in. Find the total in different ways. You could use your number bonds, partitioning, doubles or something else.

19	83	46
21	62	37
54	75	98

Subtraction grids

Let's investigate

Subtract across and down.

What do you notice about the bottom corner answer?

(a)
71	43	
58	37	

(b)
76	45	
54	25	

Work backward. Decide your bottom corner answer first.

(c)
84	45	
48	22	

(d) Make up a grid of your own. Check that the bottom corner answer is correct.

1. 36 people left a crowd of 94.
   How many people were left in the crowd?

2. Amir had $87. He spent $43.
   How much does he have left?

3. In a class of 27 children, 19 are girls.
   How many are boys?

4. Aisha had $73. She spent $38.
   How much does she have left?

5. I had 24 sweets. I ate 17 of them.
   How many do I have left?

6. I had $43. I spent $17.
   How much have I got left?

Unit 2A: Core activity 15.2 Investigating subtraction

7 A box of chocolates has 36 chocolates in it.
We ate 18 of them.

  (a) How many are left?

  (b) What fraction of the chocolates are left?

8 I had 25 marbles. I bought another 24 but lost 17 of them. How many do I have left?

9 In a class of 23 children, 12 are boys.
How many are girls?

10 I had $51.00. I spent $22.50.
How much have I got left?

11 Subtract 18 from each number in the grid.
Draw a 3 by 3 grid to record your answers in.
Find the answer in different ways. You could use your number bonds, take away too much and adjust, count back on a number line or something else.

91	87	43
62	54	78
65	26	39

Rope lengths

Let's investigate

The only way to measure lengths on Rope Island is with labelled lengths of rope. You can put two ropes end to end to measure their total, or put them side by side to find the difference.

133 m
126 m
58 m
42 m
9 m
7 m

Think about which ropes it could or could not be to make a particular length. Estimate then check.

The rope owner has lengths of 7 m, 9 m, 42 m, 58 m, 126 m and 133 m. He will only let you borrow two ropes at a time.

Which two ropes do you need to measure each of these distances?

(a) 75 m   (b) 175 m   (c) 84 m
(d) 68 m   (e) 117 m   (f) 135 m

(g) Which other lengths could you make with two ropes?

1. The aeroplane took off with 238 passengers on board.

   Nine people got off at the first stop.
   (a) How many passengers were left?
       There were seven crew members on the aeroplane.
   (b) How many people on the plane when it first took off?
   (c) How many people on the plane after the first stop?

Unit 2A: Core activity 15.3 Adding and subtracting with three-digit numbers

59

2   A bus picked up 23 people at the first stop.

19 people got on at the second stop.

Another nine people got on at the third stop.
   (a)   How many people were on the bus after the second stop?
   (b)   How many people on the bus after the third stop?
         At the stop before the final stop, 37 people got off.
   (c)   How many people got off at the last stop?

3   A shopkeeper had 14 coconuts left on Tuesday.

On Wednesday he bought two large boxes, each containing 75 coconuts.

On Wednesday he sold 31 coconuts. On Thursday he sold 34 coconuts and on Friday he sold 47 more.
   (a)   How many coconuts did he have left at the end of each day?
   (b)   How many coconuts did he sell over the three days?

4   A baker made 120 loaves of bread on Monday and sold 98.

On Tuesday he made 100 loaves and sold 87.

On Wednesday he made 130 loaves and sold 112.
   (a)   How many loaves did he make over the three days?
   (b)   How many loaves did he have to throw away each day?
   (b)   How many loaves did he throw away altogether?

Multiples of 5 and 10

1. Write the five times table, up to 10 × 5.

2. Choose two of the five times table facts to write the fact family for.

3. Choose two different facts from the five times table to draw the array for.

4. Write the ten times table.

5. Choose two of the ten times table facts to write the fact family for.

6. Choose two different facts from the ten times table to draw the array for.

Count in fives (or tens) to help you.

7. Draw a number line to show each of these multiplications and write the completed number sentence:
   - (a) 6 × 5
   - (b) 9 × 5
   - (c) 7 × 5
   - (d) 9 × 10
   - (e) 3 × 10
   - (f) 8 × 10

8. Write the multiplication and division fact family for this array.

9. Write the multiplication and division fact family for this array.

10 Copy and complete these number sentences:

(a) 8 × ? = 80 (b) ? × 5 = 25
(c) ? × 10 = 60 (d) 10 × ? = 50
(e) ? × 5 = 45

11 Copy and complete these number sentences:

(a) ? ÷ 5 = 6 (b) ? ÷ 10 = 4
(c) ? ÷ 5 = 3 (d) ? ÷ 10 = 2
(e) ? ÷ 5 = 7

12 Describe the numbers in the five times table.

Describe the numbers in the ten times table.

How are they the same? How are they different?

13 There are 27 children in a football club.

How many 5-a-side teams can they make?

14 A flower shop has 93 flowers.

How many bunches of 10 flowers can they make?

15 Write two matching calculations for this picture.

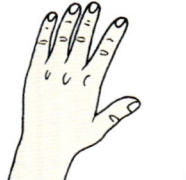

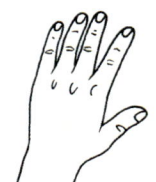

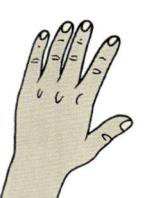

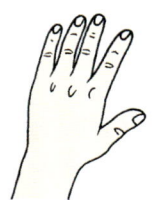

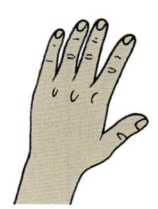

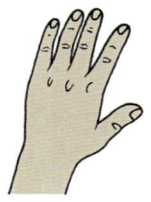

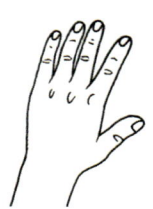

16 Write two matching calculations for this picture.

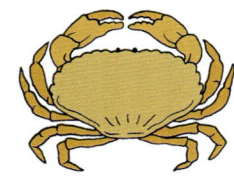

17 Write a matching story for each of these calculations.

(a) 9 × 5 = 45 (b) 3 × 10 = 30
(c) 15 ÷ 5 = 3 (d) 60 ÷ 10 = 6

More multiples

1. Write the two times table, up to 10 × 2.

2. Describe the pattern of the answers.

3. Choose two of the two times table facts to write the fact family for.

4. Choose two different facts from the two times table to draw the array for.

5. Write the four times table, up to 10 × 4.

6. Describe the pattern of the answers.

7. Choose two of the four times table facts to write the fact family for.

8. Choose two different facts from the four times table to draw the array for.

Count in twos or fours to help you.

Solve these word problems. Write the calculation that you use.

9. (a) Seven chairs are stacked in a corner. How many chair legs are left?
   (b) Three chairs are taken outside. How many chair legs are left?

10. (a) Eight birds standing on a wall. How many bird legs are there?
    (b) Five birds fly away. How many bird legs are left?

11. (a) Four lions under a tree. How many lion legs are there?
    (b) Five more lions join them. How many lion legs are there now?

12. (a) Copy and complete:
    (i) ? × 4 = 24   (ii) ? × 2 = 24
    (iii) ? × 4 = 8   (iv) ? × 2 = 8
    (v) ? ÷ 4 = 7   (vi) ? ÷ 4 = 5
    (vii) ? ÷ 2 = 1   (viii) ? ÷ 2 = 3

    (b) Choose two of these calculations to make up a story for.

Even more multiples

Vocabulary

remainder: what is left over when dividing by a particular number.

$15 \div 4 = 3$ r 3. You can make 3 groups of 4 but do not have enough to make another group of 4, so the 3 is left over. We call this the remainder.

1 (a) Write the matching times table for this number line

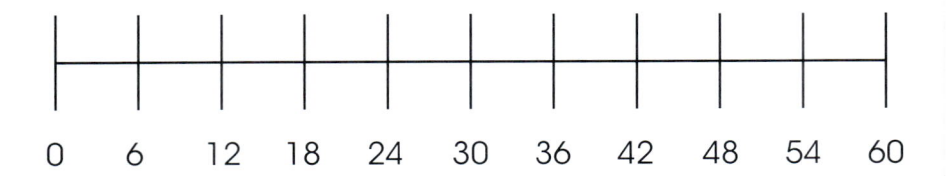

0 6 12 18 24 30 36 42 48 54 60

  (b) Choose two of the times table facts to write the fact family for.

2 (a) Write the matching times table for this number line.

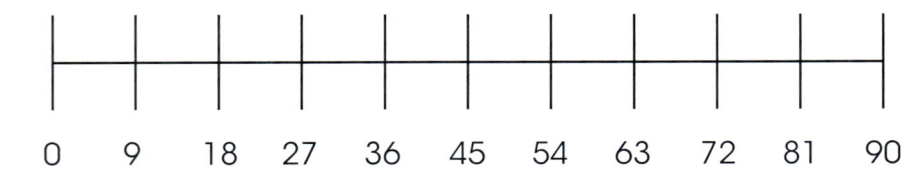

0 9 18 27 36 45 54 63 72 81 90

  (b) Choose two of the times table facts to write the fact family for.
  (c) Add the digits from each two-digit answer together.

What do you notice? Can you explain why this happens?

3 Copy and complete this table. What do you notice?

	1	2	3	4	5	6	7	8	9	10
×3	3				15					
×6	6				30					
×9	9				45					

Unit 2A: Core activity 16.3 Multiples of 3, 6 and 9

Solve these word problems. Write the matching calculation.

4   Eggs come in boxes of six. How many eggs in seven boxes?

5   Stools have three legs. How many legs on nine stools?

6   (a)   Six oranges in a bag. I buy five bags.
             How many oranges have I got?

   (b)   I give one bag to a friend.
         How many oranges have I got now?

7   (a)   There are nine bananas in each bunch.
             How many bananas in six bunches?

   (b)   I split each bunch into smaller bunches,
         each with only three bananas.

         How many bunches do I have now?

8   (a)   Copy and complete:

   (i)   ? × 3 = 27   (ii)   ? × 6 = 30
   (iii) ? × 9 = 81   (iv)   ? × 6 = 42
   (v)   ? ÷ 3 = 4   (vi)   ? ÷ 6 = 10
   (vii) ? ÷ 9 = 8   (viii) ? ÷ 3 = 7

   (b)   Choose two of these calculations to make
         up a story for.

9   Three children shared a packet of 12 biscuits.
       They had four biscuits each.

   Which calculation from question 8 matches
   this story?

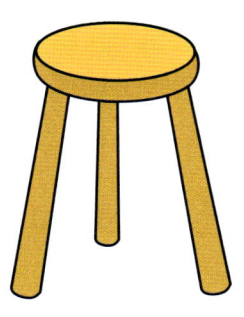

Measure

Time (2)

Let's investigate

This digital stop watch is broken

Every time it is switched on only five light bars work.

What different numbers could it show?

Investigate for other numbers of light bars.

Look at the position of the hour hand.

1 Match the times showing on the clocks.

Write the letter of the clocks that show the same times.

(a)  04:05   (b)  12:20   (c) 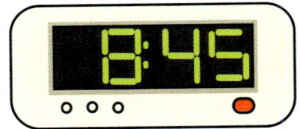 8:45

(d)    (e) 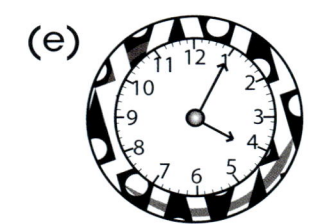   (f)

2 On each of these clocks the minute hand is missing. With a partner estimate the time by finding where the minute hand should be.

Write that time as it would be on a digital clock.

(a)    (b)    (c)

(d)    (e) 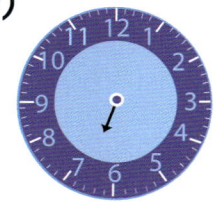   (f)

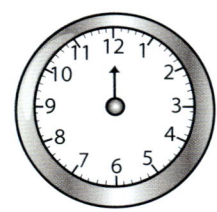

Unit 2B: Core activity 17.1 Digital clocks

Telling time

Let's investigate

You have an appointment at 2 o'clock at the dentist. Then you need to catch a train one hour after your appointment. The walk to the train station takes 20 minutes. What time will you have to leave the dentist to catch your train?

There are taxis waiting for passengers from each of these planes. They each arrive one hour before the plane is due to land.

Landing times for aircraft

Landing time	Destination	Comments
06:20	Heathrow	Landed
07:45	Paris	Delayed until 8:20
08:00	New York	Landed
10:45	Berlin	Landed
11:10	Geneva	Expected at 10:45
12:45	Amsterdam	Expected at 12:55

1. (a) How much extra time does the taxi have to wait for the passengers from Paris?
   (b) How much less time than expected does the taxi have to wait for the passengers from Geneva?
   (c) How much extra time does the taxi have to wait for the passengers from Amsterdam?
   (d) Which taxi has the longest wait? Which has the shortest?
   (e) Imagine all of the taxis are 30 minutes late arriving at the airport. What time would each taxi arrive?

2. Write down all the things you do during the day. Start from when you get out of bed in the morning. End when you are in bed at night. Show the times using either a digital or an analogue clock.

3. You need to catch two different buses to get to the shops. Bus 1 is due to leave at 2 o'clock and arrive at 2.30. You have a half hour wait between getting off the first bus and getting on the second bus.
   Bus 2 is due to arrive at the shops at 3.15.
   (a) What time is bus 2 scheduled to leave? Bus 2 leaves 15 minutes early.
   (b) (i) What time does it leave? (ii) What time does it arrive?
   Bus 1 is 15 minutes late.
   (c) What time does it arrive?

Unit 2B: Core activity 17.2 Time intervals

Days and weeks

Let's investigate

If 1 January is a Monday, how many other months have their first day as Monday too?

What if it is a Leap Year? (Hint: February will have 29 days.)

	Tue 1	Wed 2	Thu 3	Fri 4	Sat 5	Sun 6
7	8	9	10	11	12	13
14	15	16	17	18	19	20
21	22	23	24	25	26	27
28	29	30	31			

Use the calendar to help you solve these problems.

1. A packet of dog biscuits lasts six days. Ben opens a packet on Thursday the third.

   When will he open the next packet?

2. For two days every month I work in the library. I work on Tuesday and Wednesday.

   What dates could I work?

3. I had planned to visit my sister on the 31st, but she asked me to go two weeks earlier.

   When did I go?

Unit 2B: Core activity 17.3 The calendar

4   I wanted to go to the zoo on Monday 28th, but it was closed.

   I was asked to go two weeks earlier but I was busy.

   I planned to go three days after that but it was raining, so I went one week after that.

   Which day did I go to the zoo?

5   Can you un-scramble the letters to make months of the year? Put them in order starting with January.

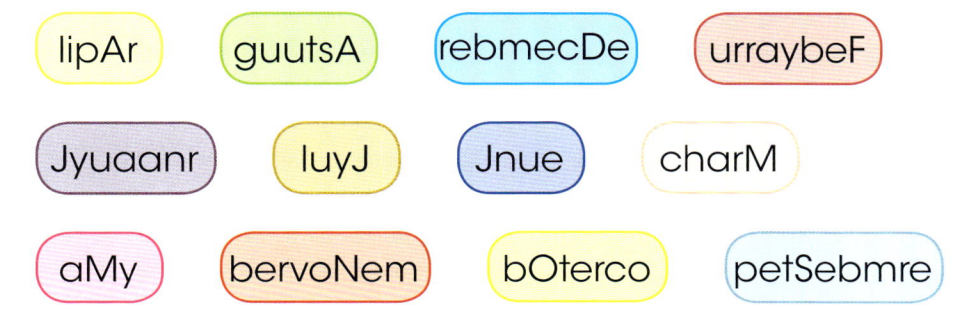

   lipAr   guutsA   rebmecDe   urraybeF

   Jyuaanr   luyJ   Jnue   charM

   aMy   bervoNem   bOterco   petSebmre

Using units

Vocabulary

approximately: almost exact or correct.

Let's investigate

Ali has a 64 gram bar of chocolate.

On day 1 he eats half of his chocolate.

On day 2 he eats half of what is left.

He does the same each day.

(a) When will he have only 1 gram left?

(b) How much would a bar of chocolate need to weigh to last Ali 14 days?

1. To find a suitable unit to measure something in, you should first estimate how big it is.

    (a) Do you think it's better to measure the distance between London and Paris in metres or kilometres?

    (b) Should an insect be measured in metres or millimetres?

    (c) Imagine a metre ruler next to a tall man. Would he be taller than 1 metre? 2 metres or 3 metres?

    (d) Is the height of a tall man likely to be 90 cm, 180 cm or 360 cm?

    (e) Is the weight of a bag of sugar about 1 kg, 10 kg or 50 kg?

2 Which unit of measurement (km, m, cm or mm) would you use for the following?
- (a) The length of your finger.
- (b) Your height.
- (c) The length of a football pitch.
- (d) The thickness of a book.

3 (a) Change 4230 g to kilograms.
- (b) Change 500 mm to metres.
- (c) Change 250 ml to litres.

4 The space between two chairs is 3 metres. Where would you put a third chair so that is in the middle?

5 My sister is $0\frac{1}{2}$ metre tall. My brother is double that height.

My gran is the same height as my brother plus 80 cm.

My dad is the same as my gran plus 20 cm
- (a) How tall is my sister in cms?
- (b) How tall is my brother in metres?
- (c) How tall is my gran?
- (d) How much taller is my dad than my sister?
- (e) (i) If my sister and my brother lay on the floor end to end, would they be the same length as my dad?
  - (ii) What would the difference in length be?

Elephants

Let's investigate

How can you weigh an elephant without using enormous elephant scales?

You can use: a boat   some bricks   the ocean

1   Use these facts to answer the questions about elephants.
   - An elephant trunk can hold about 4 litres of water.
   - Elephants eat mainly grasses, but also scrub and bark, fig leaves and fruit.
   - They eat about 150 kg of vegetation a day.
   - They drink up to 100 litres of water a day.
   - They can live up to 70 years.
   - They like to live with other elephants.

   (a)   Calculate the total amount of water that four elephants could store in their trunks at any one time.
   (b)   How many times will an elephant fill their trunk in a day?
   (c)   How much food would four elephants eat in a week?
   (d)   How much would six elephants drink in a week?
   (e)   If one elephant lives for 70 years, how long would two elephants live?

(f) (i) There are five elephants in a zoo enclosure on Monday, how much did they eat and drink?

(ii) There are four elephants in the enclosure on Tuesday, how much did they eat and drink?

Each day, an elephant leaves the enclosure to explore a nearby pasture. The number of elephants decreases by one each day.

(iii) When the enclosure is empty, how much have the elephants eaten and drunk since Monday?

(iv) On what day will the enclosure be empty?

2 A baby elephant has been born at the zoo. Lots of people sent him cards.

A sack of cards weighs 3 kg (without the sack).
Each card weighs 20 g.

How many cards were in the sack?

3 A vet checks the baby elephant's weight in August and September.

Weight in August 105 kg.

Weight in September 223 kg.

(a) How much weight did the elephant gain?

(b) He doubled his weight for the next month. How much did he weigh in October?

Money (2)

Let's investigate

Charlie divided 15 cents among four small bags.

He can use the four bags to pay any amount between 1 cent and 15 cents, without opening them.

Bag 1   Bag 2   Bag 3   Bag 4

How many cents did Charlie put in each bag?

	cost
Flower in a pot	$2.50
Bag of sweets	20 cents
A tin of beans	30 cents
A loaf of bread	$1.20

	cost
A newspaper	80 cents
A pair of gloves	$5.60
A bunch of flowers	$2.00

1. You spend exactly $5. What did you buy?

2. You give the shopkeeper $1 and get 20 cents change. What did you buy?

3. You buy two bunches of flowers. What change do you get from $5?

4. You buy a loaf of bread and a tin of beans.
   (a) How much did you spend?
   (b) How much change do you have from $5?

5. You have $10. You buy two bunches of flowers and a pair of gloves. How many bags of sweets can you buy so that you spend all of your money?

Unit 2B: Core activity 19.1 Calculating with money

6   You buy one of every item.
    (a)   How much do you spend?
    (b)   How much change do you have from $20?

7   Which would you rather have? Why?
    (a)   10 cents a week for eight weeks or 20 cents every two weeks for the same eight weeks?
    (b)   25 cents a week for 10 weeks or 20 cents every two weeks for the same 10 weeks?
    (c)   20 cents a week for 20 weeks or 30 cents every other week for the same 20 weeks.

8   How much change does each cutomer get?
    (a)   Customer 1 pays 50 cents. The item costs 17 cents.
    (b)   Customer 2 pays $1.00. The item costs 58 cents.
    (c)   Customer 3 pays $2.00. The item costs $1.28.
    (d)   Customer 4 pays $5.00. The item costs $3.45.
          You gave $2.65 change. Was that right?
          How much should you have given?
    (e)   You gave $7.89 change. Customer 5 gave you $10.00.
          How much was the item?

9   The pizza store has four different pizzas:

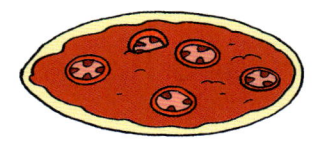

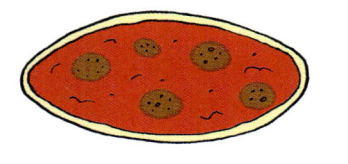

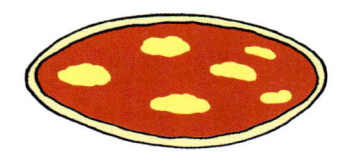

    mushroom $2.36   tomato $2.44   pepperoni $3.60   cheese $3.20

    I want to buy:
    (a)   Half a tomato and half a cheese pizza. How much will it cost?
    (b)   Half a mushroom and half a pepperoni. How much will it cost?
    (c)   A whole cheese and half a mushroom. How much will they cost?
    (d)   A tomato and cheese pizza and half a tomato pizza. How much will they cost?

At the zoo

Let's investigate

Last weekend I was given my pocket money.
It is meant to last me all week.

On Monday, I spent a quarter of my money on clothes.

On Tuesday, I spent one half of my remaining money on a CD.

On Wednesday I spent half of my remaining money on sweets.

Finally, on Thursday, I spent my last $1.50 on a comic.

How much pocket money did I receive?

The school bus has arrived at the zoo.

All the children hold hands with one other child.

They all have some money to spend, but they don't all have the same amount of money.

Answer these questions.

1. Piara has $7.75 and Ranjit has $4.50.

   How much money do they have together?

2. After buying some oranges for $7.00, Gopal has $3.25 left.

   How much money did Gopal have to begin with?

3. Ibrahim has $6.75 and Malik has $2.25.

   How much more does Ibrahim have than Malik?

4   Ayesha has $6.00 and Nashreen has $3.50.

How much more does Ayesha have than Nasreen?

5   After buying some pencils for $6.01, Rach has $4.00 left.

How much money did Rach have to begin with?

6   After buying some peanuts for $4.34, Compton has $2.00 left.

How much money did Compton have to begin with?

7   Bianca has no money left. Larissa gives her $3.75 for a drink and some biscuits.

Larissa started with $8.00. How much does she have left?

8   At the zoo shop three sweets are on special offer.

A Sparkle, a Chewy and a Nibbler together cost 40c.
- A Nibbler is over three times the price of a Sparkle.
- Six Sparkles are worth more than a Chewy.
- A Nibbler, plus two Sparkles costs less than a Chewy.

What is the price of each sweet?

Liquid measures

Let's investigate

You are camping, and have an 8-litre bowl which is full of fresh water.

You need to share this water fairly into exactly two portions
(4 + 4 litres).

But you only have two empty bowls: a 5-litre and a 3-litre bowl.

Divide the 8 litres in half.

Explain how you would do that.

This bottle holds 1 litre of water.

A millilitre is about 20 drops of water.
There are 1000 millilitres in a litre.

1. Mr Poulter filled a bucket with water to clean his floor.

   Would his bucket hold 9 litres or 9 millilitres of water?

2. A cook adds half of a teaspoon of vanilla to her cake recipe.

   Did she use 2.5 l or 2.5 ml of vanilla?

3. Maria bought a cup of hot chocolate.

   Does her cup hold 400 litres or 400 millilitres of hot chocolate?

4. Andrea bought fruit juice for her friends to drink at her birthday party.

   Would she buy 5 l of juice or 5 ml?

5. Your teacher has a large fish tank in her office.

   Does her fish tank hold 100 litres or 100 ml of water?

6. Which would you rather buy, a 2 litre bottle of fruit juice that costs $2.50 or 6 × 300ml cartons of fruit juice which cost 50c each? Why?

7. (a) Max buys six donuts and a 300ml carton of juice for $3.50.
   Susie buys four donuts and two 300ml cartons of juice for $3.00.
   Ben buys eight donuts and five 300ml cartons of juice for $6.50.
   How much is one donut? How much is one carton of drink?

   (b) At the end of the day the café was selling food and drink cheaply.
   Max buys six donuts and a 300ml carton of juice for $2.50.
   Susie buys four donuts and two 300ml cartons of juice for $2.75.
   Ben buys eight donuts and five 300ml cartons of juice for $4.00.
   Who got best value for money if each item costs 50c on its own? Why?

Handling data

Venn diagram

Vocabulary

Venn diagram: a way of sorting things according to their different features.

1. **(a)** The labels are missing from this Venn diagram. What would you write on the new labels? Explain why.

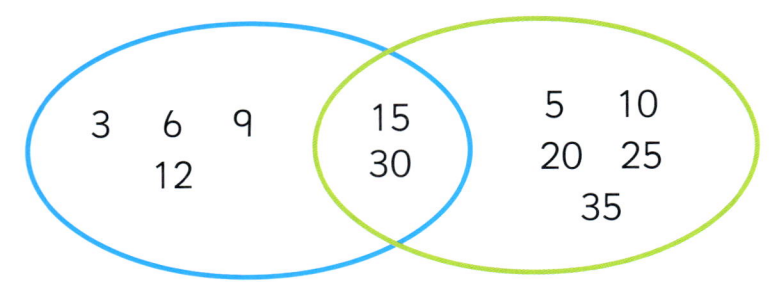

   Left circle: 3, 6, 9, 12
   Intersection: 15, 30
   Right circle: 5, 10, 20, 25, 35

   (b) Copy the Venn diagram and add in the numbers 13, 14, 16, 17, 18, 19, 45. Explain why some of the numbers are outside the circles.

2. These children are playing a game. They are using large hoops to sort themselves into as many different groups as they can.

   (a) What labels would you put on this diagram?
   (b) Draw some Venn diagrams and sort the children in as many different ways as you can.

   Put labels on your Venn diagrams.

   How many different ways can you sort them?

Unit 2C: Core activity 20.1 Venn diagrams

3 Draw and complete your own Venn diagram, but leave off the labels.

Give your diagram to a friend. What labels would they put on?

Were they the same as you were thinking?

Tallying

Let's investigate

Throw a dice 10 times and record the numbers you throw.

Make a tally chart to record how many times each number on a dice is thrown.

Number	Tally
1	
2	
3	
4	
5	
6	

Which number was thrown the most? How many times?

Do you think that number will be thrown the most if you throw the dice 20 times?

Make another tally chart, then throw the dice 20 times.

Which number did you throw most often? How many times did you throw it?

Which number did you throw least? How many times did you throw it?

What differences are there between the two tables?

Repeat the investigation. Do you get the same results?

1 Use the tally chart to answer the questions in this quiz.

The graph shows the number of books collected by each student.
   (a) How many books does Jon have?
   (b) How many books does Phillip have?
   (c) How many books do Kev and Vicki have together?
   (d) What is the total number of books?

	Books
Jon	|||| |||| |||| ||
Clare	||||
Vicki	|||| |||| |||
Kev	|||| |||| |||| ||||
Phillip	|||

Unit 2C: Core activity 20.2 Tallying

2 Make a tally chart to show the information below.

What is your favourite hobby?

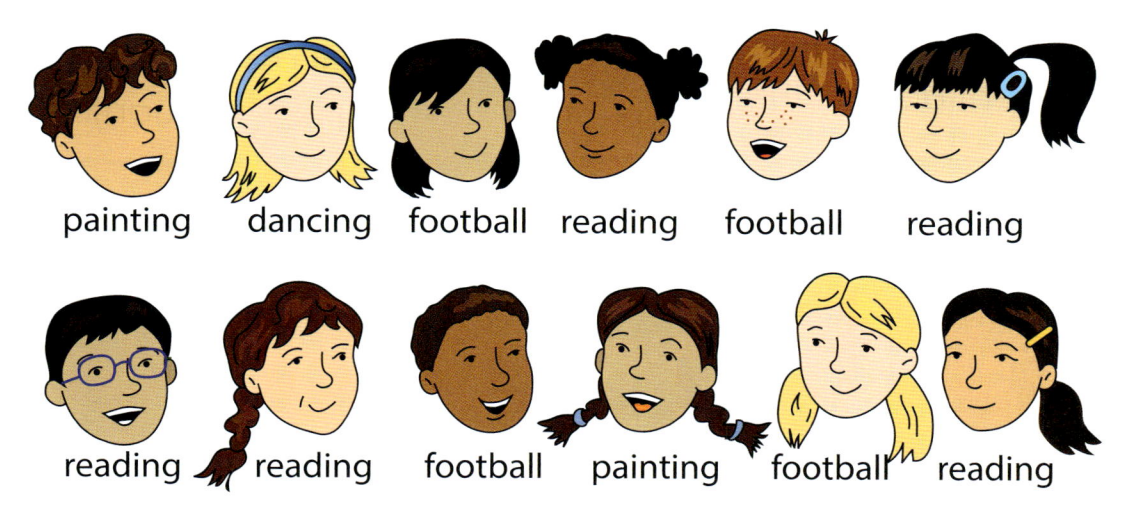

painting   dancing   football   reading   football   reading

reading   reading   football   painting   football   reading

3 Use this **bar graph** to make a tally chart.

Number of children

Type of pet	2	4	6	8	10
dogs					
cats					
fish					
rabbits					
turtles					

83

Pictogram

> **Vocabulary**
>
> **pictogram:** a graph that uses pictures to represent quantities.

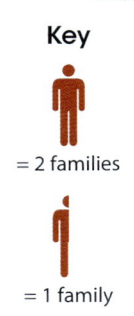

1 This pictogram shows how many families visited the zoo on different days of the week.

Key

👤 = 2 families

👤 = 1 family

(Pictogram showing families visiting the zoo — x-axis: Monday, Tuesday, Wednesday, Thursday, Friday, Saturday, Sunday)

(a) On what day were there no families?
    Why do you think this was?

(b) Which day was the most popular for visiting the zoo?
    Why do you think this was?

(c) What was the difference between the number of families on Friday and Saturday?

(d) Can you give some reasons why there was such a difference in the number of families on those two days?

(e) What was the total number of visitors over this week?

(f) Twice the number of families visited the following week. How many would that be?

(g) Draw a pictogram to show that number of visitors.

Unit 2C: Core activity 20.3 Pictograms and bar charts

2 This pictogram shows the amount of sunshine over three days.

(a) (i) How many hours of sunshine were there in total over the three days?

Monday	☼ ☼ ☼ ☼
Tuesday	☼ ☼ ☼ ☼ ☼ ☼ ☼
Wednesday	☼ ☼ ☼ ☼ ☼ ☼ ☼ ☼ ☼ ☼

Key ☼ = 1 hour sunshine

(ii) How many hours of sunshine were there over Monday and Tuesday?

(iii) How many more hours of sunshine were there on Wednesday than on Monday?

(b) This pictogram shows the same information but the key is missing.

Write the key.

Monday	☼ ☼
Tuesday	☼ ☼ ☼ ☼
Wednesday	☼ ☼ ☼ ☼ ☼

3   The minibeast house at the zoo wanted to find out about favourite minibeasts.

The visitors completed a survey. This is what they found.

Favourite minibeasts

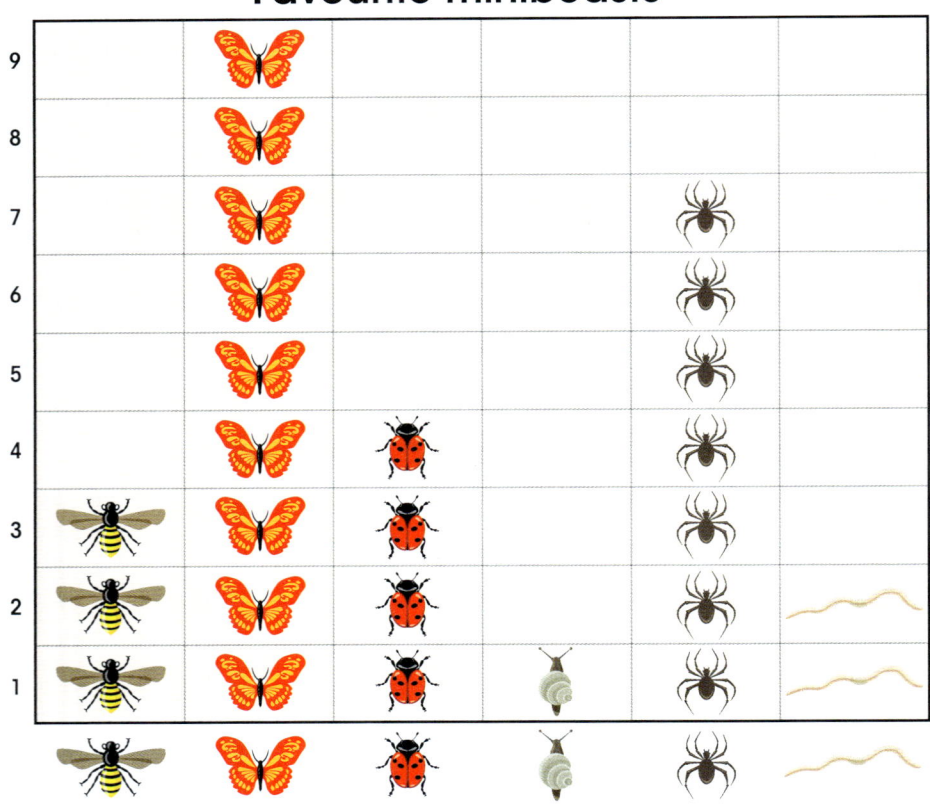

(a) Which was the favourite minibeast? How many people liked it?
(b) Which was the least favourite minibeast?
(c) If you had room for only four new tanks, which two minibeasts would you not have? Explain why.
(d) How many people answered the survey?

4   A café asked some customers about their favourite ice cream flavours. This is what they found out.

> - 12 people like vanilla ice cream.
> - Three more than that like chocolate ice cream.
> - Six people like strawberry ice cream.
> - 11 people like lemon.
> - The favourite ice cream is mint. It has the same number as strawberry and lemon together.

(a) Make a bar chart to show this information.

(b) I want to buy two ice creams. I want the most popular flavour. My friend likes the least popular. Which ice creams will I buy?

5   Draw two bar charts showing the same information but using different keys.

They could show ways to come to school, games you like to play or food you like to eat.

Number

Order, order!

Let's investigate

The numbers below have been put in order.

Copy and complete by filling in the missing numbers.

There are lots of different correct answers.

(a) 42, 57, ?, 74, ?.

(b) 75, ?, 124, ?, 189.

(c) 82, ?, ?, 98, ?, 142.

(d) 93, ?, 65, ?, ?, 21.

(e) ?, 234, ?, ?, 327 ?.

(f) 762, ?, ?, 543, 326, ?.

1 Copy the table, rounding each number to the nearest 10.

47	63	79	24
9	15	54	81
28	91	30	75
70	4	46	72

Remember the rule for rounding, 5 Up.

2 Copy the table, rounding each number to the nearest 100.

327	643	489	629
200	123	274	753
309	472	891	912
450	975	651	568

Remember the rule for rounding, 50 Up.

Unit 3A: Core activity 21.1 Comparing, ordering and rounding

3   Give three examples to match each statement:
    (a) When you round a number to the nearest ten, there are no ones in the answer.
    (b) When you round a number to the nearest 100, there are no tens or ones in the answer.
    (c) When you double an odd number, the total is always even.
    (d) The order in which you add two numbers does not matter.

4   Use < or > to make these statements correct
    (a) 23 ? 45, 45 ? 23
    (b) 56 ? 65, 65 ? 56
    (c) 67 ? 82 ? 94
    (d) 81 ? 59 ? 37
    (e) 45 ? 56 ? 54
    (f) 78 ? 63 ? 75

5   Write each set of numbers in order, from the smallest to the largest.
    (a) 271, 254, 207, 248, 275, 269.
    (b) 147, 386, 261, 258, 174, 318.
    (c) 534, 517, 478, 491, 543, 415.

6   Now write these sets of numbers in order, from the largest to the smallest.
    (a) 378, 362, 303, 327, 343, 382.
    (b) 146, 834, 539, 163, 734, 541.
    (c) 509, 519, 591, 915, 951, 905.

Times ten

1 Copy the grid, multiplying each number by 10.

24	78	41	12
97	35	85	81
31	68	59	19
72	47	62	92

2 Write a number sentence for each problem and work out the answer.
   (a) What is eight multiplied by 10?
   (b) What is 10 lots of 30?
   (c) Which number is 10 times bigger than 63?
   (d) Each bag holds six sweets.
       How many sweets in 10 bags?
   (e) I have 10 pieces of string, each 42 cm long.
       How much string do I have altogether?
   (f) Ten cups of water hold 50 ml each.
       How much water in the cups?
   (g) A school has 10 classes, each with 27 children in.
       How many children in the school?
   (h) There are 15 cakes in a box.
       How many in 10 boxes?
   (i) Pencils cost 13c each.
       How much would 10 pencils cost?

3   Copy and complete these number sentences
   (a) 23 × 10
   (b) 89 × 10
   (c) 37 × 10
   (d) 52 × 10
   (e) 74 × 10

4   When you multiply a two-digit number by 10, there are no ones in the answer.

   True or False? How do you know?

5   Each purse has some 1c coins in it. If each 1c coin was swapped for a 10c coin, how much money would be in each purse?

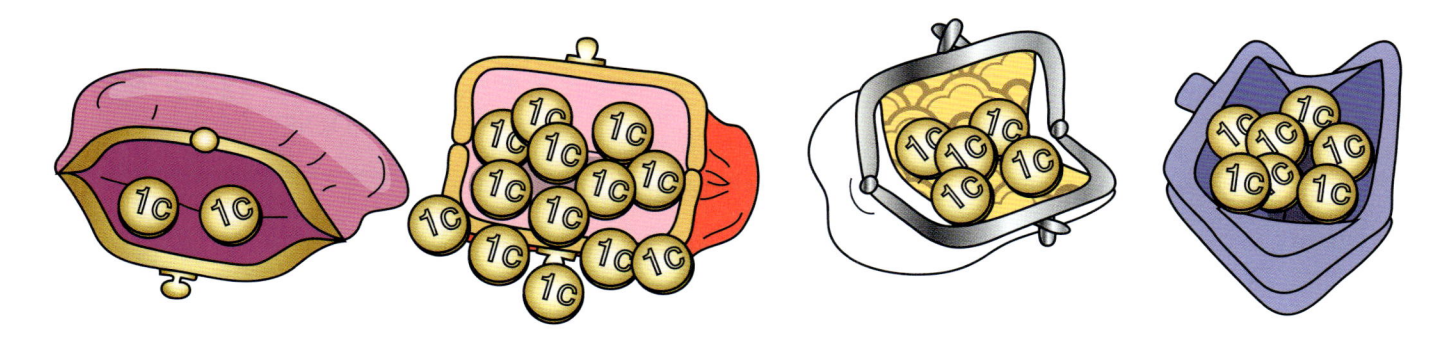

6   If the coins in each purse were swapped for coins worth ten times as much, how much money would be in each purse?

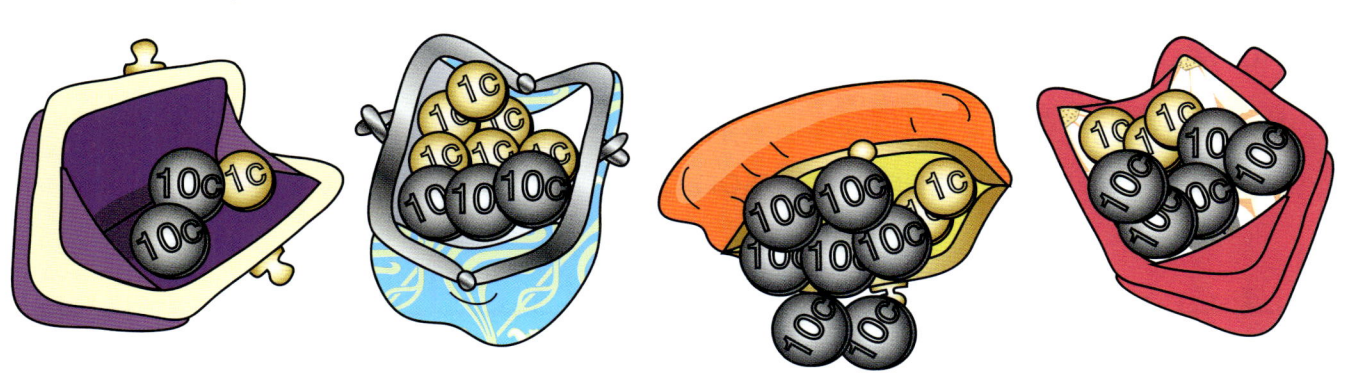

Fraction trios

Let's investigate

These cards show $3\frac{1}{2}$ in three ways.

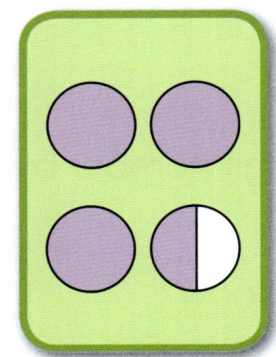

[Card 1: $3\frac{1}{2}$] [Card 2: 7 halves] [Card 3: three full circles and one half circle]

Show the following mixed numbers in three different ways.

You do not have to draw circles.

$2\frac{1}{2}$, $4\frac{3}{4}$, $6\frac{1}{4}$, $8\frac{1}{2}$, $9\frac{3}{4}$.

Choose another number of your own to show in three different ways.

1. Which is bigger, nine halves or nine quarters?

   How do you know?

2. How many quarters in $5\frac{3}{4}$?

3. If you shared five apples between two people, how many apples would each person get?

4. If you shared six apples between four people, how many apples would each person get?

Vocabulary

half: one of two equal sized parts of a whole.

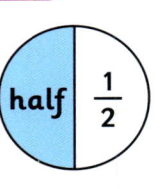

quarter: one of four equal sized parts of a whole.

fraction: part of a whole.

mixed number: a number which has whole numbers and a fraction, for example $2\frac{1}{2}$.

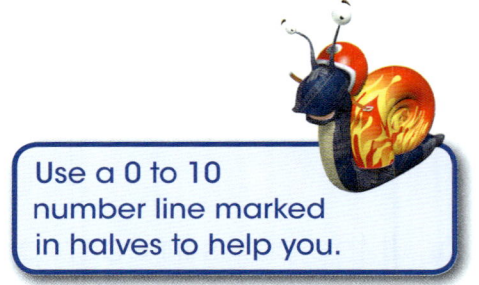

Use a 0 to 10 number line marked in halves to help you.

5 How many quarters in $8\frac{1}{4}$? How do you know?

6 Which is bigger three halves or five quarters?
   How do you know?

7 Which is bigger, $\frac{3}{4}$ or $\frac{1}{2} + \frac{1}{4}$?

8 How many halves in $7\frac{1}{2}$?

   What is an easy way to work it out?

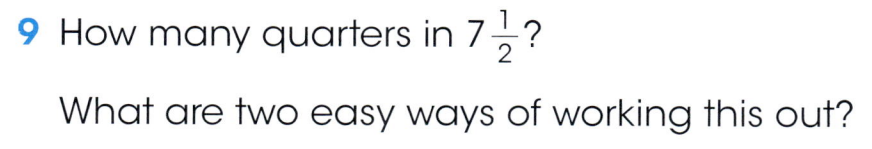

   Use a 0 to 10 number line marked in quarters to help you.

9 How many quarters in $7\frac{1}{2}$?

   What are two easy ways of working this out?

10 How many $\frac{3}{4}$ in $4\frac{1}{2}$?

    What is an easy way to work it out?
    Will this always work?

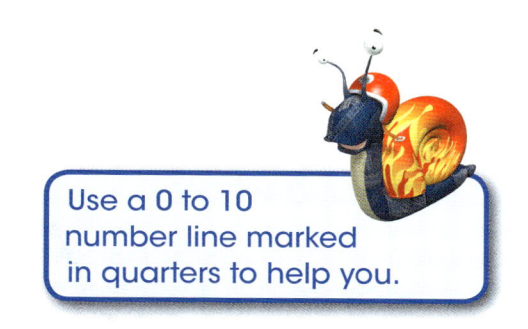

Fraction wall

Vocabulary

one third, thirds:
$\frac{1}{3}$ one of three equal parts of a whole.

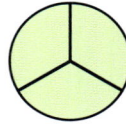

one eighth, eighths:
$\frac{1}{8}$ one of eight equal parts of a whole.

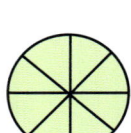

one tenth, tenths:
$\frac{1}{10}$ one of ten equal parts of a whole.

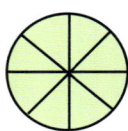

Use counters to help you divide.
Finding a fraction of something is division.

To help you divide, get the right number of counters and share them using that line of the fraction wall.
So for 12 ÷ 4, get 12 counters and share them onto the four quarters.
Each quarter will have three counters on it, so 12 ÷ 4 = 3.

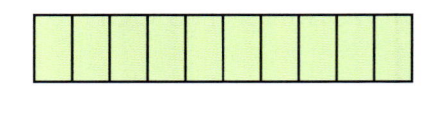

1										
$\frac{1}{2}$					$\frac{1}{2}$						
$\frac{1}{3}$			$\frac{1}{3}$				$\frac{1}{3}$			
$\frac{1}{4}$		$\frac{1}{4}$			$\frac{1}{4}$			$\frac{1}{4}$		
$\frac{1}{8}$	$\frac{1}{8}$	$\frac{1}{8}$	$\frac{1}{8}$	$\frac{1}{8}$	$\frac{1}{8}$	$\frac{1}{8}$	$\frac{1}{8}$			
$\frac{1}{10}$	$\frac{1}{10}$	$\frac{1}{10}$	$\frac{1}{10}$	$\frac{1}{10}$	$\frac{1}{10}$	$\frac{1}{10}$	$\frac{1}{10}$	$\frac{1}{10}$	$\frac{1}{10}$	

Use the fraction wall to help you answer the questions opposite.

1 Which is bigger $\frac{2}{3}$ or $\frac{5}{8}$?

2 Which is smaller, $\frac{6}{8}$ or $\frac{8}{10}$?

3 Express the following fractions in a different way:
   (a) $\frac{1}{4}$ = ?   (b) $\frac{3}{4}$ = ?   (c) $\frac{1}{2}$ = ?

4 $\frac{1}{3} > \frac{3}{8}$. True or false?

5 $\frac{2}{3} < \frac{7}{10}$. True or false?

6 Write four statements about the fraction wall using <.

7 Write four statements about the fraction wall using >.

8 What is $\frac{1}{4}$ of 12?

9 What is $\frac{1}{3}$ of 15?

10 What is $\frac{3}{4}$ of eight?

11 What is $\frac{6}{10}$ of 20?

12 What is $\frac{5}{8}$ of 40?

13 What is 24 ÷ 3?

14 What is 9 ÷ 3?

15 What is 32 ÷ 8?

16 What is 24 ÷ 4?

17 What is 20 ÷ 10?

18 What is 16 ÷ 8?

19 Would you rather have $\frac{1}{3}$ or $\frac{3}{10}$ of a cake?

20 Would you rather have $\frac{1}{2}$ of $3 or $\frac{3}{4}$ of $2?

21 Would you rather have $\frac{3}{8}$ or $\frac{4}{10}$ of a pizza?

22 Would you rather have $\frac{6}{8}$ of $4 or $\frac{5}{8}$ of $6?

Fraction posters

Some children made a poster about $\frac{1}{3}$.

Ask your teacher for a large piece of paper. Choose a fraction and make your own fraction poster. Show your fraction in as many different ways as you can. You could work on your own or with a partner.

$\frac{1}{3}$ of 24 is 8, so 24 ÷ 3 = 8

12 ÷ 3 = 4 so $\frac{1}{3}$ of 12 is 4

Here are some problems for you to solve:

1. If I cut a piece of paper in half, then in half again and in half again, what fraction of the whole is each piece?

2. The fraction shop sells cakes in any fraction.

   One day, customers bought $\frac{5}{8}$, $\frac{1}{2}$, $\frac{1}{4}$, $\frac{5}{10}$, $\frac{2}{3}$, $\frac{2}{8}$, $\frac{1}{3}$ and $\frac{3}{4}$.

   How much cake did the shop sell altogether?

3. The clothes shop has a special offer on.

   All prices are reduced by $\frac{1}{10}$.

   A $10 T-shirt now costs $9.
   (a) How much will a $40 coat cost?
   (b) What about a $60 pair of shoes?

   The clothes sale is not going well, so the owner is going to reduce prices by $\frac{2}{10}$ instead of $\frac{1}{10}$.
   (c) How much is the T-shirt now?
   (d) How much is the coat now?
   (e) How much are the shoes now?

Unit 3A: Core activity 22.3 More fractions

Double (and half) trouble

Play with a partner. One of you uses the first page, the other one uses the second page.

Take it in turns to ask each other a double or half question, using the numbers on the page.

If this is your page, you might ask, '*What is double 50?*' You put a counter on 50 and your partner puts a counter on 100 on their page.

If your partner does not have the answer number, you miss that turn and must remove your counter.

Can you put a counter on every number?

Which sets of numbers are on each page? Which numbers are missing from the set?

	5	300	14	
90	12	70	9	350
3	10	50	2	60
250	7	400	15	150
8	30	13	18	16
80	100	1	20	17
500	19	40	16	450
	4	200	11	

Solve these problems by doubling or halving.

1. Ali and Huan have seven marbles each.

   How many marbles altogether?

2. Ali and Huan have eight sweets each.
   - (a) How many sweets altogether?
   - (b) Ali eats half of his sweets.
     How many sweets altogether now?

3. I have a piece of string 50 cm long.

   When I cut it in half, how long is each piece?

Use the patterns of multiples that you know.

Double (and half) trouble

If this is your page, you might ask, 'What is half of 700?' You put a counter on 700 and your partner puts a counter on 350 on their page.

Put a counter on each number as you use it. If your partner does not have the answer number, you miss that turn and must remove your counter.

Can you put a counter on every number?

Which sets of numbers are on each page? Which numbers are missing from the set?

4 It takes $1\frac{1}{2}$ hours to get home.

If I walk twice as fast, how many minutes will it take?

5 The bus has 56 seats.

How many seats in two buses?

6 A bottle of squash makes 32 drinks.
 (a) How many drinks from two bottles?
 (b) How many from $\frac{1}{2}$ bottle?

	45	900	10	
500	16	34	200	38
4	28	5	26	600
25	36	400	8	30
100	12	50	15	22
24	35	32	800	6
18	700	20	14	300
	2	1000	40	

98

Complements to 100

Use this blank 100 square to help you work out complements to 100.

(a) Find the complement to 100 for each of these numbers:

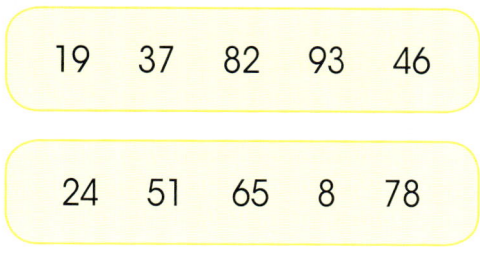

> 19   37   82   93   46

> 24   51   65   8   78

Write the number sentence first, for example:

19 + ? = 100, then rewrite the number sentence with the correct number instead of a box.

(b) Write a subtraction fact for each calculation.

Use the blank 100 square to help you. Or you could draw a number line or a thought line.

1. Write the number sentences for these complements to 100 thought lines.

    (a) ? ? 3 ? 50 ? 53
    (b) ? ? 5 ? 30 ? 35
    (c) ? ? 1 ? 20 ? 21
    (d) ? ? 8 ? 70 ? 78
    (e) ? ? 6 ? 10 ? 16
    (f) ? ? 7 ? 60 ? 67

Use complements to 100 to solve these problems.

2. There are 100 books on the bookshelf.
   23 are borrowed.
   How many are left on the shelf?

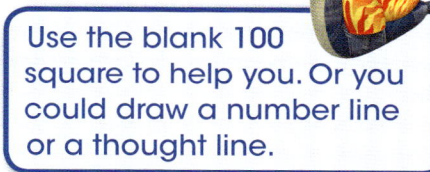

Unit 3A: Core activity 24.1 Complements to 100

99

3 There are 100 sweets in a packet.

67 are given out at a party.

How many are left?

4 Sanjay had $100.

He spent $38.

How much did he have left?

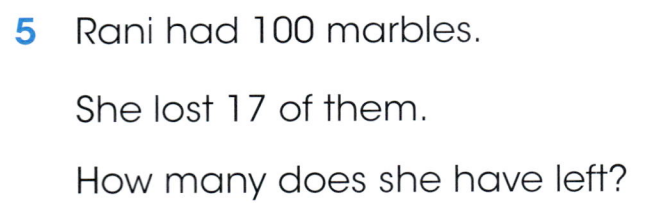

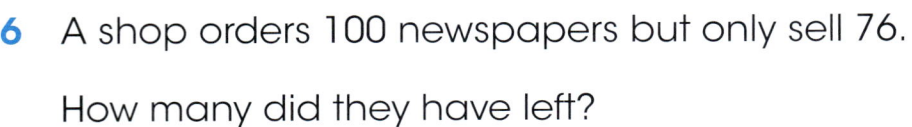

5 Rani had 100 marbles.

She lost 17 of them.

How many does she have left?

6 A shop orders 100 newspapers but only sell 76.

How many did they have left?

7 43 cm is cut off 1m of string.

How much string is left?

8 There are 100 flowers on the plants in the garden.

36 are picked.

How many flowers are left in the garden?

9 There are 100 tissues in a box.

13 are used in a week.

How many are left?

10 There are 100 pencils in a pack.

23 children are given four each.

How many are left?

11 There are 100 oranges for sale on a market stall.

67 are sold. Five have gone bad and have to be thrown away.

How many are left?

12 There are 200 sweets in a jar.

13 packets of 10 sweets are given out.
(a) How many sweets are left?
(b) How many packets?

13 I have a piece of wood 3 m long.

I cut off a piece 234 cm long.

How much wood is left?

14 Tami had $200.

She spent $178.

How much does she have left?

15 Rashid had $300.

He spent $215.

How much does he have left?

Add or subtract?

1. Here are four dominoes from a set.

    Use the dominoes as two-digit numbers.

    Add or subtract any two numbers.

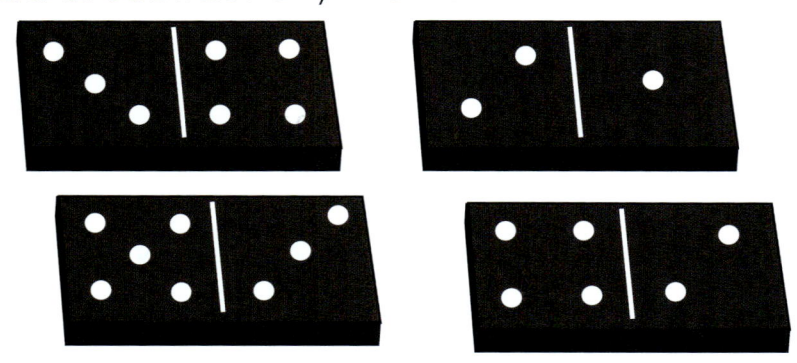

    How many different answers can you find?

    What is the smallest answer?

    What is the largest answer?

2. Choose a number from each grid.

    Add the first pair of numbers, subtract the next pair and so on until you have used all the numbers.

123	438	91
519	74	346
87	252	65

2	9	6
7	5	3
4	1	8

3. A bus picks up 16 people at the first stop.

    At the second stop, 23 people get on and seven people get off.

    At the third stop 19 people get off and eight people get on.
    - (a) How many people are on the bus after the second stop?
    - (b) How many people are on the bus after the third stop?

Sums and differences – target 1000

1. Choose a number from each box.

   Work out the sum and difference of your pair of numbers, then add them together.

   Choose another pair of numbers and repeat.

   Add the totals together.

   The aim is to get as close to 1000 as you can.

   Can you make a total of exactly 1000?

76	23	61	49
33	72	14	25
56	51	38	69
17	92	43	84

74	96	12	52
68	36	27	47
58	79	41	63
32	18	83	21

Vocabulary

sum: the answer to an addition calculation. So for 23 + 19 = 42, 42 is the sum.

difference: how much bigger or smaller one quantity or number is than another.

Find pairs to make the highest total until your total is over 800, then think carefully about which pairs of numbers to use.

2. Copy and complete the grid.

		sum	difference	sum + difference
10	20	30	10	40
20	30	50	10	
30	40			
40	50			
50	60			
60	70			
70	80			
80	90			
90	100			

   What patterns have you noticed?

Much multiplication

Vocabulary

open array: rectangle used to support multiplication and division.

```
        12
    ┌────────┬──┐
  5 │        ┊  │
    │   50   ┊10│
    └────────┴──┘
       10     2
```

Let's investigate

Look at this method of working out the nine times table:

$1 \times 9 = 10 - 1 = 9$

$2 \times 9 = 20 - 2 = 18$

(a) Copy and complete the nine times table up to 10×9.

(b) Describe the pattern this shows in the nine times table.

1 Copy and complete each table.

× 3	
5	→ 15
	→ 21
	→ 27
	→ 39

× 4	
	→ 16
	→ 28
10	→
	→ 48

× 6	
	→ 18
5	→
	→ 42
	→ 54

2 Copy and complete each multiplication square.

×	2			
		9	12	
5			20	
		27		

×		6		
			36	
6			54	
			50	60

3 Copy and complete. Draw an open array to help you.

(a) 16×2 (b) 23×3 (c) 17×4

(d) 14×5 (e) 15×6 (f) 13×9

4 A number multiplied by six is 24. What is the number?

5 A number multiplied by four is 32. What is the number?

6 A number multiplied by nine is 63. What is the number?

7 What is nine times as big as four?

8 How many times larger than 24 is 240?

9 How many days are there in five weeks?

10 How many 10c coins in $4?

11 Seven children wear boots. How many boots altogether?

12 I am nine. My mother is five times older than me. How old is she?

13 I have six pens. My friend has three times as many. How many pens does he have?

14 There are six eggs in a box.

How many eggs in 14 boxes?

Use an open array to help you.

15 You need three eggs to make a cake. How many eggs to make seven cakes?

16 Four friends each had five sweets. How many sweets altogether?

17 Five monkeys each have six bananas.

How many bananas altogether?

18 Cans of lemonade cost 35c each.
They are sold in boxes of 10.
How much does a box cost?

19 How many legs do eight dogs have?

20 How many legs for 10 sheep, one sheep dog and a shepherd?

21 There are 12 eggs in a box.

How many eggs in three boxes?

Use an open array to help you.

22 Four classes in a school have 23 children each. The other four classes each have 18 children.

How many children in the school?

23 If you roll two dice and multiply the numbers together, the highest score is 36, 6×6.

Which numbers below 36 are impossible to score?

24 If you rolled three dice and multiply the numbers together, what are the highest and lowest possible totals?

25 Make up a story for each of these number sentences.
- (a) $5 \times 10 = 50$
- (b) $9 \times 2 = 18$
- (c) $12 \times 5 = 60$
- (d) $8 \times 3 = 24$

26 Give four examples to show whether each statement is true or false:
- (a) Multiplying numbers in a different order does not change the answer.
- (b) A multiple of three is always a multiple of six.
- (c) A multiple of four is always a multiple of two.
- (d) All the numbers in the four times table are odd.

Multiplying and dividing

Let's investigate

(a) Copy and complete the table.

(b) What do you notice about the numbers either side of the line? Why is that?

×	2	3	4	5	6	9	10
2	4						
3							
4							
5				20			
6							
9							81
10							

1. What happens to numbers when you multiply by one?

2. What happens to numbers when you multiply by 0?

3. Copy and complete each table.

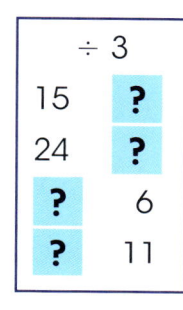

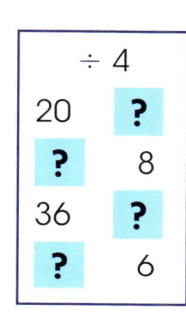

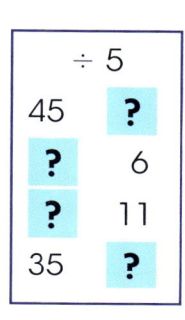

   ÷ 3: 15 → ?, 24 → ?, ? → 6, ? → 11

   ÷ 4: 20 → ?, ? → 8, 36 → ?, ? → 6

   ÷ 5: 45 → ?, ? → 6, ? → 11, 35 → ?

4. Write four different × and ÷ facts for each group of numbers.
   (a) 3 30 10   (b) 7 28 4   (c) 8 48 6   (d) 9 63 7

5. Copy and complete:
   (a) 18 ÷ ? = 2   (b) 40 ÷ ? = 8   (c) 36 ÷ ? = 6   (d) 42 ÷ ? = 6
   (e) ? ÷ 10 = 3   (f) ? ÷ 6 = 5   (g) ? ÷ 3 = 9   (h) ? ÷ 4 = 3

6. Five children share 40 sweets between them equally. How many sweets does each child get?

7. A tray of plants hold six plants. How many trays can be filled from 66 plants?

8. Give three examples to show whether each statement is true or false.
   (a) If a number has five ones, it divides exactly by five.
   (b) All odd numbers can be divided exactly by two.

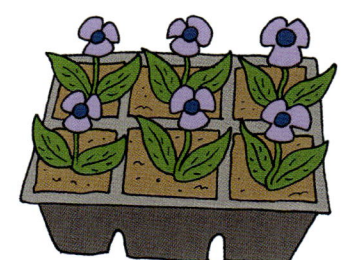

9. Make up a story for each of these number sentences
   (a) 36 ÷ 4 = 9   (b) 100 ÷ 2 = 50   (c) 48 ÷ 4 = 12

Unit 3A: Core activity 25.2 Division with open arrays

What does a remainder mean?

1. Copy and complete
   - (a) 37 ÷ 4 =
   - (b) 16 ÷ 3 =
   - (c) 26 ÷ 6 =
   - (d) 17 ÷ 2 =
   - (e) 29 ÷ 4 =
   - (f) 22 ÷ 6 =
   - (g) 49 ÷ 9 =
   - (h) 47 ÷ 5 =

2. Copy and complete
   - (a) ? ÷ 6 = 6 r 2
   - (b) ? ÷ 3 = 4 r 2
   - (c) ? ÷ 2 = 7 r 1
   - (d) ? ÷ 5 = 12 r 3
   - (e) ? ÷ 4 = 7 r 2
   - (f) ? ÷ 3 = 9 r 1
   - (g) ? ÷ 10 = 7 r 6
   - (h) ? ÷ 9 = 4 r 3

> Read the question carefully to see if the remainder means that you need to round up or down one more.

Think carefully about any remainders when problem solving.

3. A car can carry five people. 37 people need transport.

   How many cars are needed?

4. A relay team has four runners.

   How many teams can you make with 18 runners?

5. A baker makes 54 cakes. Five cakes fit in each box.

   How many boxes will he need?

6. Four children can sit at a table.

   How many tables are needed for 26 children?

7. Four monkeys share 25 bananas equally.

   How many whole bananas does each monkey get?

8 There are 28 marbles in a set. Six children are playing. How many marbles do they get each?

9 How many teams of four can be made from a class of 30 children?

10 (a) How many 30 cm lengths of string can be cut from a metre of string?
 (b) How long is the piece left over?

11 A tray of plants hold six plants. How many trays can be filled from 50 plants?

12 Ten children can sit on each bench. How many benches are needed for 37 children?

13 There are 46 tennis balls. Each box holds four balls. How many boxes are needed for the balls?

14 224 children are going on a trip. Each bus holds 50 children. How many buses are needed?

15 Each child in question 14 needs a notebook. Notebooks are sold in packs of 10.

How many packs are needed?

16 I have $22. Books cost $4.
 (a) How many books can I buy?
 (b) How much change will I get?

17 There are 93 cans of lemonade. A box holds nine cans. How many boxes do I need?

18 Make up a story for each of these number sentences:
 (a) $17 \div 3 = 5\text{ r }2$ (b) $23 \div 4 = 5\text{ r }3$
 (c) $56 \div 6 = 9\text{ r }2$ (d) $49 \div 5 = 9\text{ r }4$

Geometry

Right angles

Let's investigate

These squares all have right angles.

The squares are made of matchsticks.

Can you take away three matchsticks and still have three squares?

Remember they must all have right angles.

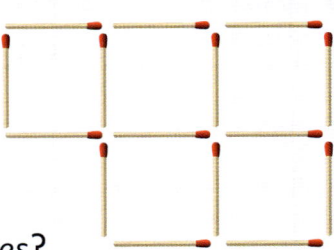

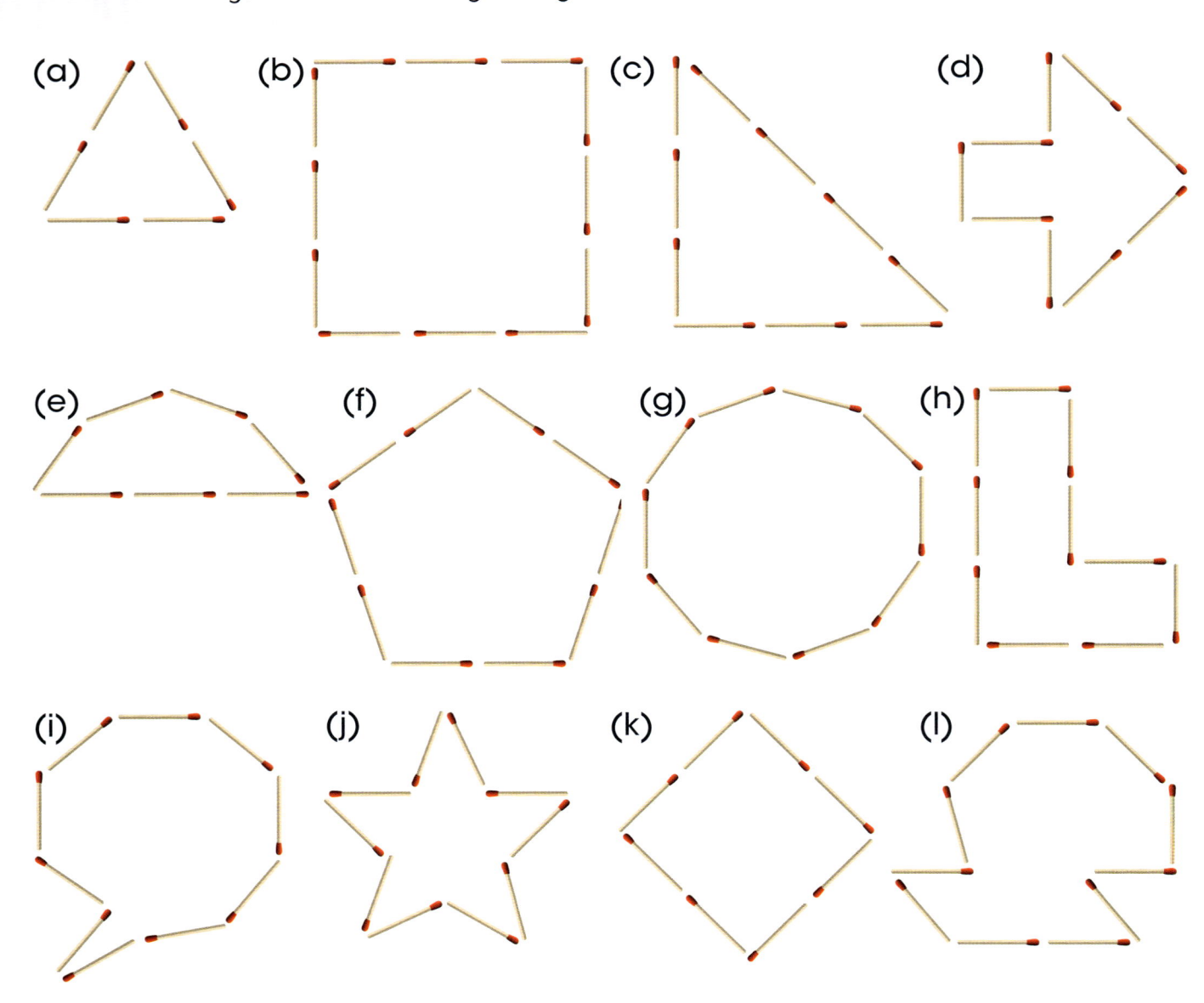

(a) (b) (c) (d)

(e) (f) (g) (h)

(i) (j) (k) (l)

Unit 3B: Core activity 26.1 Finding and drawing right angles

1. Draw the shapes that have one or more right angles

2. How many right angles are there all together?

3. Draw as many regular 2D shapes that have one or more right angles as you can.

4. Draw as many regular 3D shapes that have one or more right angles as you can.

5. What would happen if there were no right angles?

6. Draw a house with no right angles.

7. Choose something different to draw that has no right angles.

Symmetry (2)

Let's investigate

How many times can you fold a piece of paper in half and cut shapes out?

Investigate different ways of folding and cutting the paper.

1. Find all the lines of symmetry for these regular polygons.

   Write a rule about the number of lines of symmetry for regular polygons.

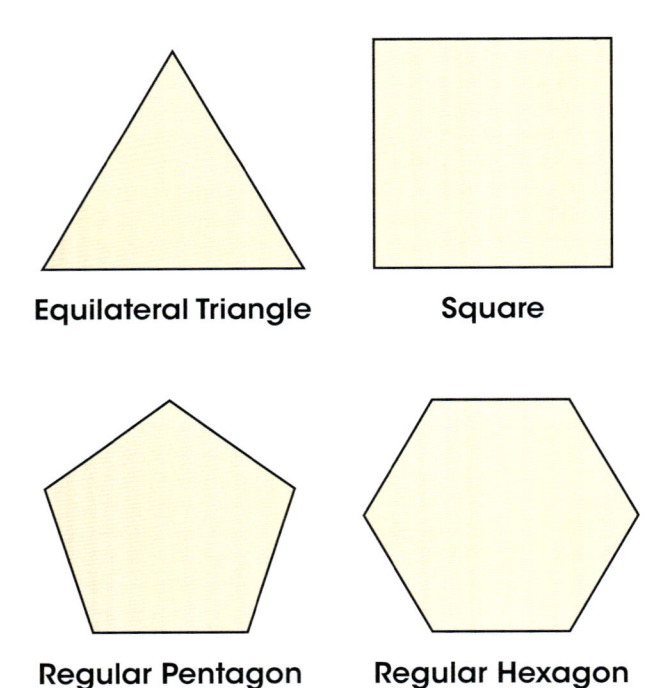

   Equilateral Triangle

   Square

   Regular Pentagon

   Regular Hexagon

2. Which of these figures has a line of symmetry?

   Draw the ones that have and show the line of symmetry.

   (a)    (b)    (c)

   (d) 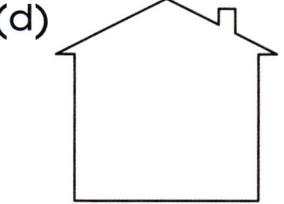   (e)

3. Is the line drawn a line of symmetry for the figure?

   (a) 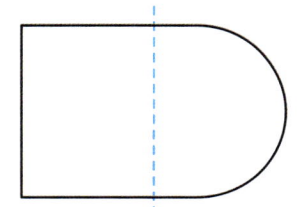   (b) 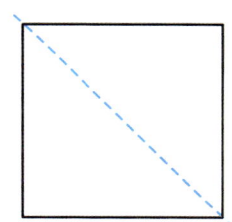   (c)

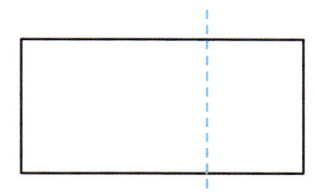

   (d) 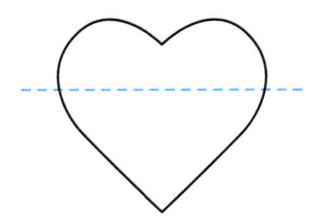   (e) 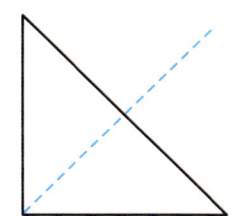   (f)

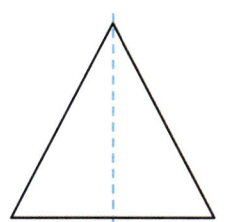

113

Symmetry (3)

Let's investigate

Draw a 5 by 5 grid and colour the squares.

Use as many colours as you can but the grid must be symmetrical.

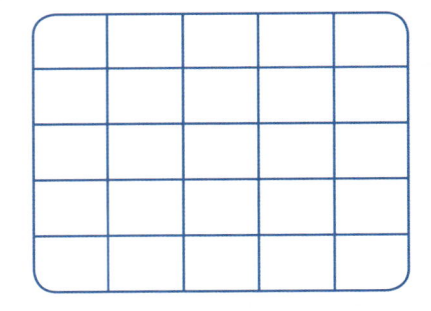

What's the most number of colours you can use?

Try with 3 × 3 grid, or a 7 × 7 grid.

1. Find the flags which have exactly two lines of symmetry?

   Copy them and draw in the lines of symmetry.

   United Kingdom   USA   Switzerland   Scotland

   Syria   Bahamas   Cameroon   Spain

   Trinidad and Tobago   Finland   Libya   Kazakhstan

   Niger   Panama   Somalia   Macedonia

114

Unit 3B: Core activity 27.2 Identifying symmetrical shapes

2   Copy these shapes.

Sketch the shapes along the line of symmetry.

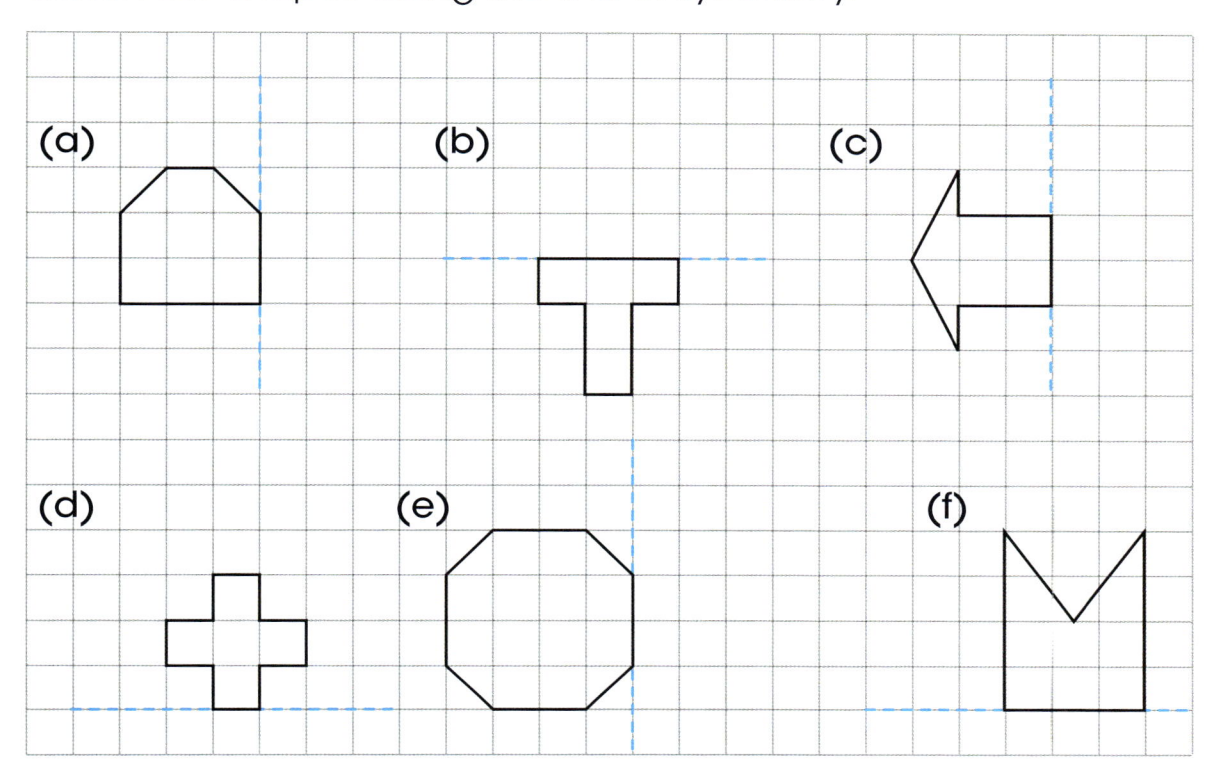

(a)   (b)   (c)

(d)   (e)   (f)

3   My hen has started to lay strange eggs.

Copy the eggs and complete the design in the line of symmetry.

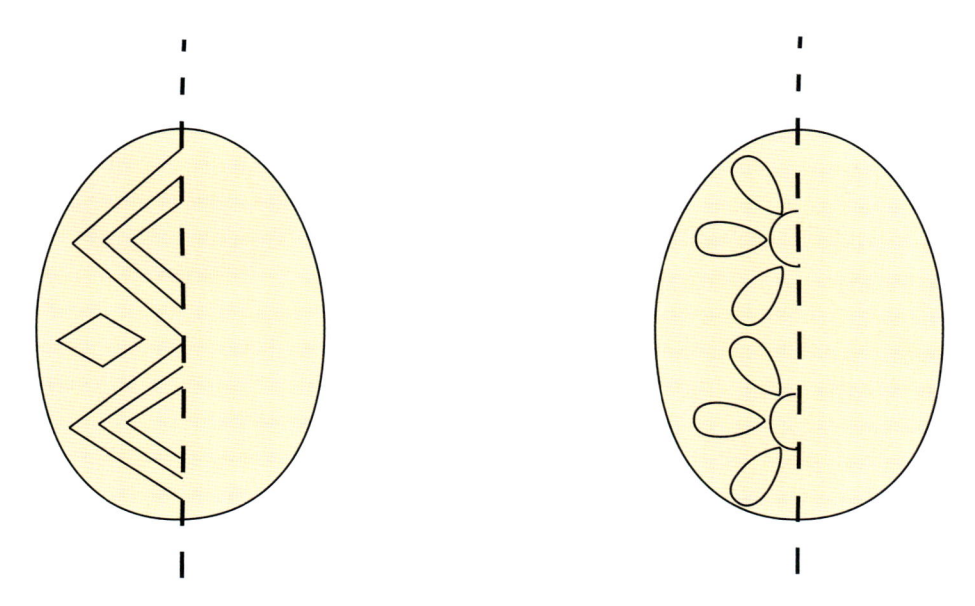

Draw a symmetrical egg of your own.

Position and movement

Let's investigate

A frog can jump over one other frog of a different colour onto an empty rock or it can slide onto an empty rock which is immediately next to it.

Only one frog at a time is allowed on each rock.

A frog cannot move backwards.

What is the least number of moves for the frogs to changes places?

What if there are two frogs on each side?

Or three frogs each side?

Look for a pattern in the number of moves.

1   Answer these questions.
   (a) Face north, turn clockwise one right angle. Which way are you facing?
   (b) Face east, turn clockwise half a turn. Which way are you facing?
   (c) Face west, turn anti-clockwise five right angles. Which way are you facing?
   (d) Face north, turn anti-clockwise two right angles. Which way are you facing?
   (e) Face south, turn two right angles clockwise, three right angles anti-clockwise and one right angle clockwise. Which way are you facing?

2 Copy and complete the sentences.

The first one is done for you:
- (a) The book is next to the teddy bear.
- (b) The car is _____ the windmill.
- (c) The ball is _____ the doll and the giraffe.
- (d) The boat is _____ the giraffe.
- (e) The teddy bear is at the _____ .
- (f) The blocks are at the _____ .

3 Write instructions to get the bird to the worm.

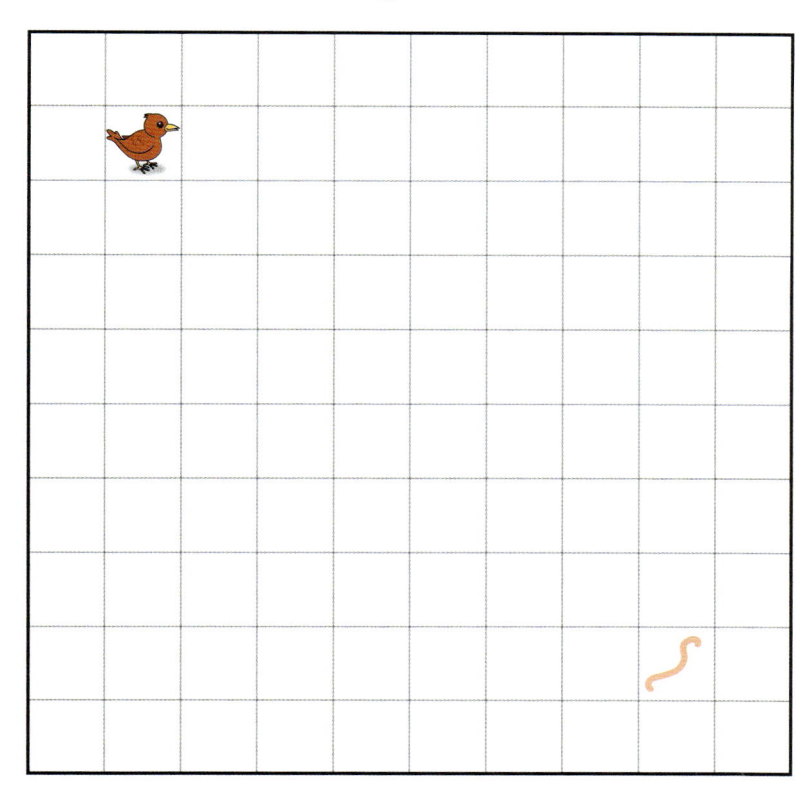

Using coordinates

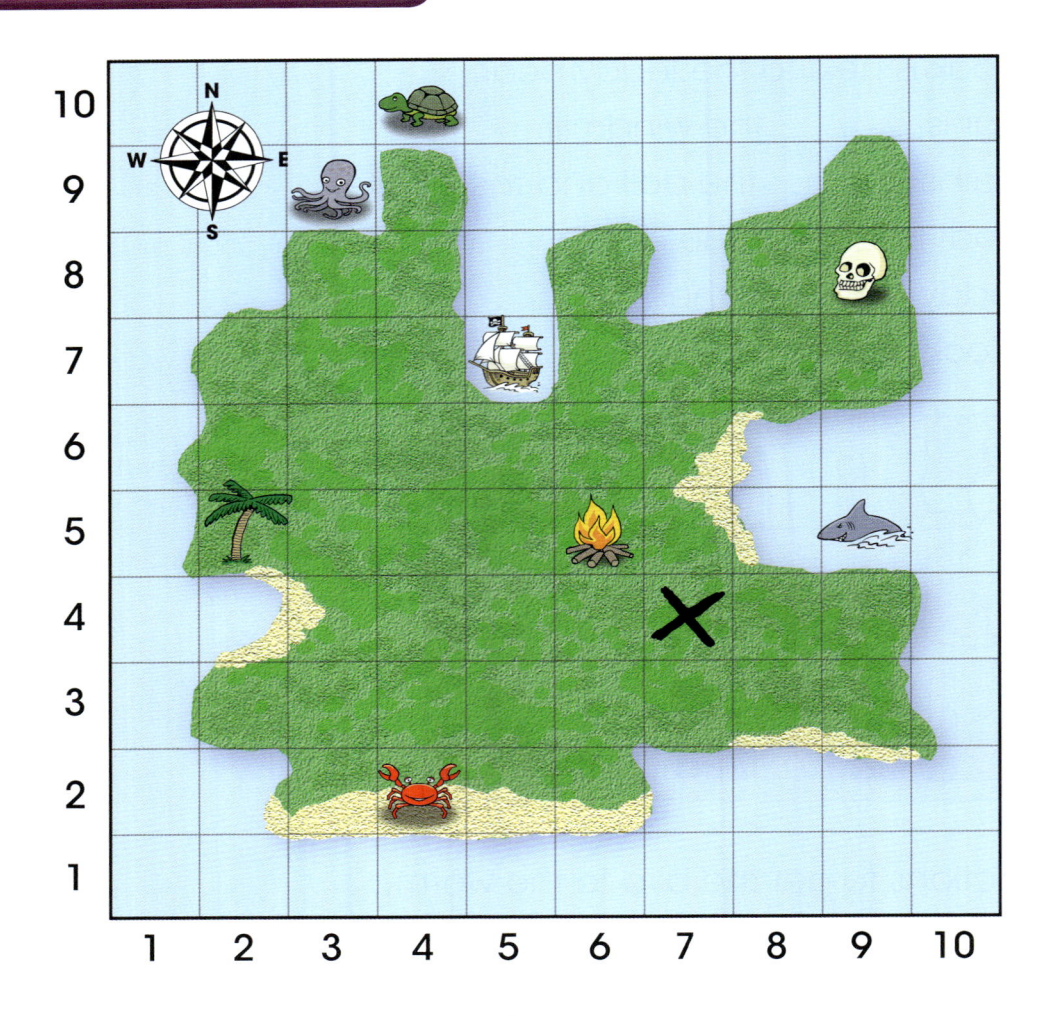

1. What is at square (3, 9)?

2. Write down the coordinates of the shark.

3. Lucky Jim is standing at the palm trees on the west of the island.

   He moves four squares east.

   Where is he now? Give the coordinates of the square.

4. You are standing at the skull.

   You want to get to the treasure marked X.

   Write the instructions to get you there.

   Start like this: Move one south to (9, 7)

5. The crab and the turtle start walking at the same time.

   The turtle moves south.

   The crab moves north.

   They walk at the same speed.

   Where will they meet? Give the coordinates.

6. Start at the crab's original position.

   Stop when you come to water and change direction to stay on land.

   Plot your route round the island until you reach the treasure.

   Keep a record of your movements. Start like this: Move two east to (6, 2)

7. Copy these patterns.

   Make them symmetrical about the mirror line.

   Write down the coordinates of each square you colour, and what colour you use.

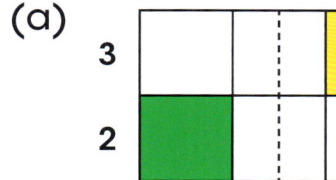

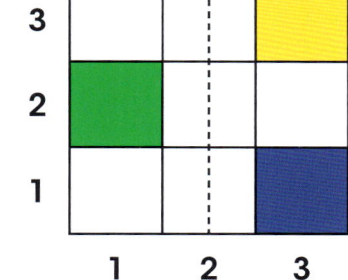

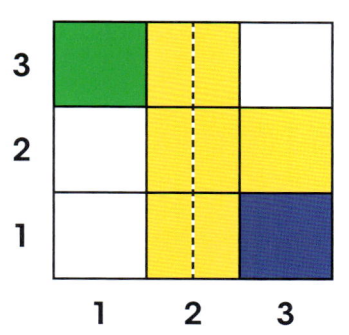

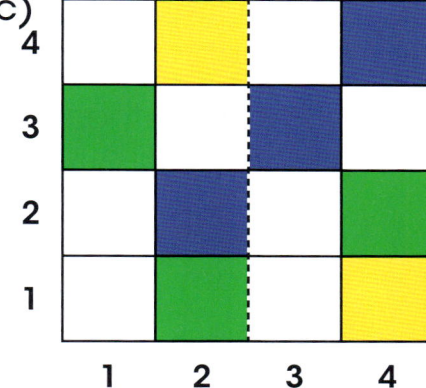

8. Write the coordinates to make this picture.

   Record them in a table like this one.

   Make a picture of your own on squared paper.

   Write the coordinates.

Black	
Blue	
Red	
Grey	
Brown	

Measure

Passage of time

Let's investigate

Joseph is playing in the woods with his friends.

To find out where each other is they flash their torches.

Joseph sees two lights flash at the same time. The first of them flashes every fourth second and the other flashes every fifth second.

How many times do they flash together during a whole minute?

Work out these answers. Write the time and show it on an analogue and digital clock.

1. Halina stopped at Jack's Soup, Salad and Sandwich café for lunch.

    She stayed there until she had to leave to meet her friend, Roz, at the library.

    They were meeting at 1:30 pm. The library is a 20-minute walk from Jack's.

    What time did Halina have to leave the restaurant in order to get to the library right on time?

2   Mateus and Bruno are going to join a parade on Saturday.

They have to be at the parade an hour before it starts.

The parade starts at 11:30 am.

If it takes 25 minutes to walk to the starting point of the parade, what time will they have to leave home in order to be there on time?

3   Betty, the owner of Betty's Buns, has to bake 12 large pans of chocolate buns before she leaves for the day.

She can bake two pans of buns at a time.

Betty knows that for perfect buns each pan must bake for 15 minutes – no more, no less.

If she starts baking at 05:45, what is the earliest she can close the shop?

4   Rosalie has a busy day planned today.

She will meet her friend, Vernon, at the fair.

That is a 15 minute walk from home.

They will stay at the fair for an hour.

Then they will take a 10 minute walk over to the park.

The first thing they will do there is to buy a pie from Pete's pie van.

If Rosalie left home at 09:30, what time did she and Vernon buy their pie?

Time puzzles

Let's investigate

Some of the light bars on this clock are not working.

What times might the real time be?

1. My friend and I can't seem to get our watches working properly.

   His (watch A) consistently runs one minute per hour fast, and mine (watch B) runs two minutes per hour slow.

   We both set our watches so they are correct at 12:00.
   - (a) If the real time is 12:00, what time does watch A say?
   - (b) When watch A says 01:01, what is the real time?
   - (c) When watch B says 3:52, what does watch A say?
   - (d) If the real time is 04:00, what does Watch B say?

     Copy and complete the table to help you.

Real time	Watch A	Watch B
12:00		
01:00		
02:00		
03:00		
04:00		
05:00		
06:00		

2. Annie didn't like to tell her age, so when she was asked, her mother answered for her.

   Her mother said, "I am double her age plus 10. In 10 years' time she will be half my age."

   How old is Annie?

   Clue: Work with even numbers.

   Clue: She is less than 16.

3   A snail climbs up a slippery wall.

The wall is 30 cm high. Each minute the snail climbs 5 cm, but slides back 4 cm.

How many minutes will it take the snail to reach the top of the wall?

4   There is a water-barrel with three different water-taps.

With the small tap the water-barrel can be filled in 20 minutes.

With the medium the tap the water-barrel can be filled in 12 minutes.

With the large tap the water-barrel can be filled in five minutes
- (a) I have six minutes to spare and want the barrel to be half full. Which tap should I use?
- (b) Which tap will half fill the barrel in 10 minutes?
- (c) Which tap will fill the barrel quickest?
- (d) How much quicker does the large tap fill the barrel than the small tap?
- (e) I have two barrels, each with their own medium tap. If I turn both taps on at the same time, how long will it take to fill both barrels?

5   One hen lays two eggs in three days.

How many eggs do three hens lay in nine days?

Money (3)

The pocket money rule:

In our house we have a rule for pocket money.

Each day:

7 year olds will get 7 cents a day

8 years olds will get 8 cents a day

9 year olds will get 9 cents a day

10 year olds will get 10 cents a day

11 year olds will get 11 cents a day.

How much money will a child from each age group get in the next 14 days?

Show how you worked out the answer.

You have been given some money to buy new clothes:

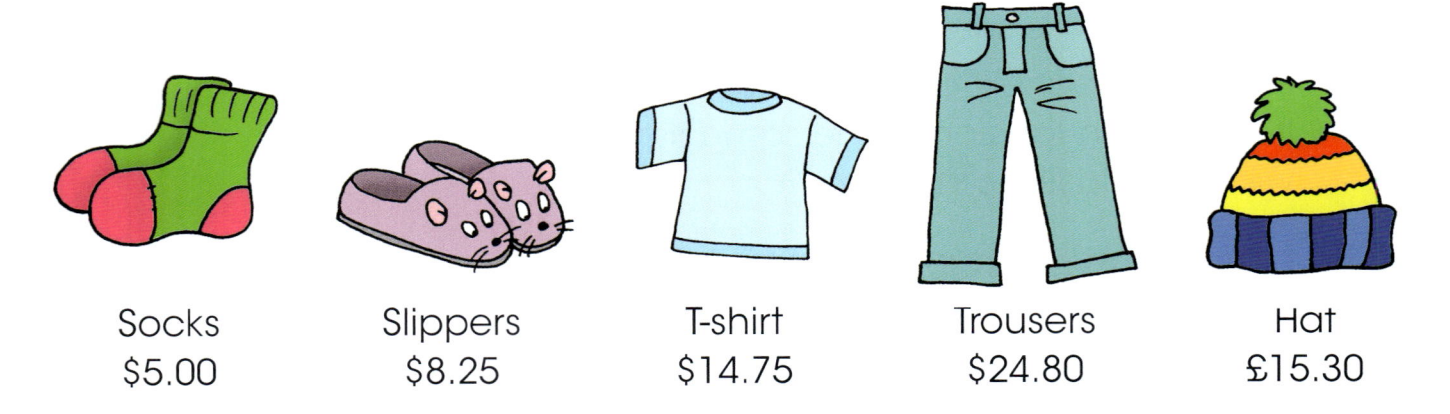

Socks	Slippers	T-shirt	Trousers	Hat
$5.00	$8.25	$14.75	$24.80	£15.30

1   You have $10. What can you buy?

2   You have $20. What can you buy?

Unit 3C: Core activity 30.1 Adding and subtracting money

3 You had $30 and you have change of $2.00.

What did you buy?

4 You have $50.00.

What do you buy and what change do you get?

5 You have $30.00.

Can you buy a T-shirt and a hat? Explain your answer.

Copy and complete the receipts:

1 Dave's Department Store

Book	$1.50
Toy doll	$3.00
TOTAL	
CASH	$5.00
CHANGE DUE	

2 Dave's Department Store

Packet of crisps	60 cents
Bottle of water	80 cents
Cheese sandwich	$1.50
TOTAL	
CASH	$5.00
CHANGE DUE	

3 Dave's Department Store

Drum	$15.00
Flute	$5.00
TOTAL	
CASH	$30.00
CHANGE DUE	

4 Dave's Department Store

Teddy bear	$12.00
Toy car	$1.50
TOTAL	
CASH	$20.00
CHANGE DUE	

5 Dave's Department Store

Chocolate bar	80 cents
Apple	60 cents
Pineapple	$2.00
TOTAL	
CASH	$5.00
CHANGE DUE	

6 Dave's Department Store

Xylophone	$13.00
Recorder	$2.50
TOTAL	
CASH	$50.00
CHANGE DUE	

Money puzzles

Let's investigate

Which would you rather have:

- Your length in 20 cent coins side by side

  OR

- Your height in 1 cent coins stacked one on top of each other?

Why? Explain your reason.

1. Pencils from the shop cost 25 cents each.

   How much would it cost for everyone in your class to have a pencil?

2. I save 4 cents a day from the first of January.
   - (a) On what day will I have $2.00?
   - (b) On what day will I have $200.00? (Imagine there are no leap years)

3. Take three coins from a dollar.

   What are you left with? What are the largest and smallest amounts?

4 I saw a jacket for $97. I didn't have enough money so I borrowed $50 from my dad and $50 from my mum.

I now had $100.

I bought the jacket and had $3 change.

I gave my dad $1 and my mum $1 and kept the other dollar for myself.

Now I owe my dad $49 and my mum $49

I worked it out that $49 + $49 = $98

$98 plus my $1 = $99.

Where is the missing $1?

5 Three men went to a restaurant for lunch. When they went to the counter to pay, the owner placed a box down in front of them, and ordered the first man to put all the money in his pocket into the box, and take 2 dollars out for the bus.

The owner then told the second man to put in as much as what was now left in the box, and take 2 dollars for the bus.

Finally, the owner told the third man to put in as much as what was now left in the box, and take 2 dollars for the bus.

The owner then went and looked in the box, and to his surprise, nothing was there!

How much money did the first man put into the box?

Capacity

Let's investigate

A bath holds 286 litres. A shower uses 137 litres.
I have a shower and my sister has a bath.

How much water will we save if my sister decides to have a shower instead?

1. How much water is in this measuring jug?

2. A jug holds 2 litres of juice.
   (a) How many 150 ml cups of juice can be filled from the jug?
   (b) How much juice will be left in the jug?

3. (a) Which jug contains more water, A or B?
   (b) How much more does it contain?
   Explain how you worked it out.

4. Peter poured some water out of a litre jug.

   Look how much is left in the jug.

   Estimate how much water is left.

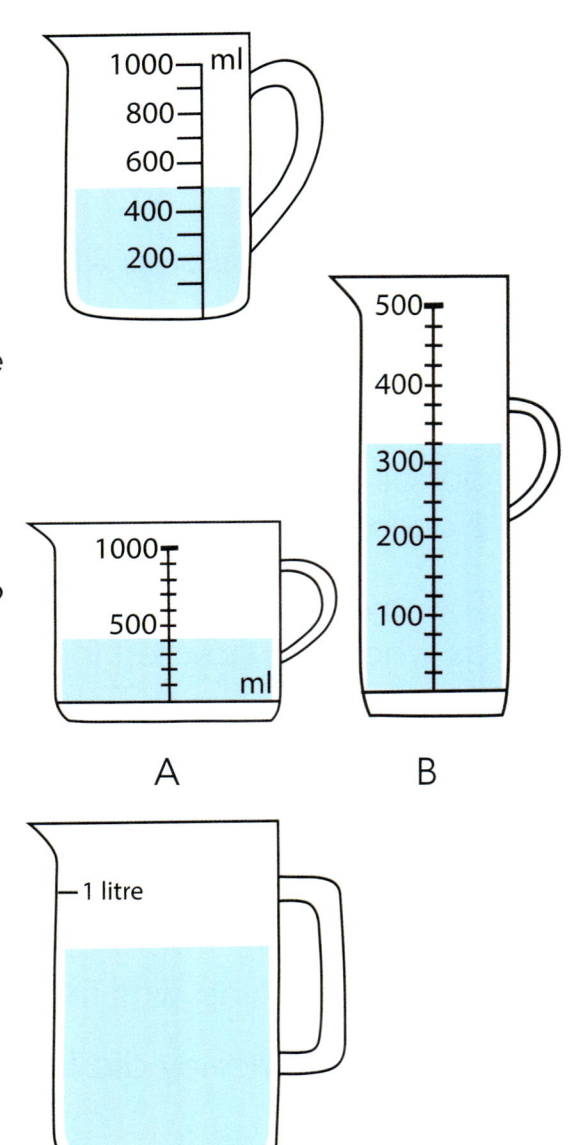

5 A can of cola holds 100 ml

  (a) How much will four cans hold?

  (b) How many more cans would I need to make a litre?

6 A jar has 358 ml of jam.

  (a) My grandma uses 198 ml to make some jam tarts. How much is left?

  (b) If my mum needs 645 ml of jam to make a cake, how much more jam will we need?

7 I make a 750 ml pot of tea. I pour 136 ml into a cup and another 245 ml into a mug.

How much tea is left in the pot?

8 Thomas collected some rain water in a bucket. The bucket holds 6.5 litres.

  (a) Stephen used 3.5 litres to water some plants. How much is left?

Next time they use a 7000 ml bucket to collect the same amount of rainwater.

  (b) How much more rain is needed to fill this bucket?

Length

Let's investigate

Amy and Betty are snails. They live on a wall.
They can only travel along the edge of the bricks.
Each brick is 30 cm long and 15 cm wide.

Amy wants to visit Betty.

How far is the shortest route keeping
to the edges of the bricks?

Is there more than one way to go?

1   Winston and Conrad are twins. Winston is 100 cm tall.
    Conrad is 1 metre tall. Who is taller?

2   Gulab likes to go fishing. He holds the record for the longest fish.

It was 82 cm long. His friend Habib likes to fish too.

The longest fish he has caught is 18 cm long.

How much shorter was his fish than Gulab's?

3   Mandisa is 155 cm tall, Ebere is 180 cm tall, Juma is 185 cm tall.
   (a) What is the total of Mandisa and Juma's height?
       Write your answer in centimetres and in metres and centimetres.
   (b) How much shorter is Mandisa than Juma?
   (c) What is the total of all three children's heights?
       Write your answer in centimetres and in metres and centimetres.

4 (a) What is the difference between 53 and 36 cm?
   (b) Draw a line that length.

Measuring

Let's investigate

I think that three times round your head is approximately the same as your height.

What do you think?

How could you find out?

Explain what you would do.

1. Copy the table below.

    Follow these instructions and complete the table.
    - (a) Stretch your arms out wide. Measure from the tip of your longest finger across to the tip of the same finger on the other hand. Write that distance down.
    - (b) Measure the length of your foot. Write the measurement down.
    - (c) Measure your height. Write it down.
    - (d) Measure from your wrist to your elbow. Write the measurement down.

I measured	It measured
My arm span	cm
My foot length	cm
My height	cm
From wrist to elbow	cm

2   Answer these questions
   (a) My height is approximately the same as _____ of my foot lengths.
   (b) My height is approximately the same as _____ .
   (c) My foot length is approximately the same as _____ .

3   In the 1986 Olympics the high jump record was 2.45 metres.
   (a) How high is that in cm?
   (b) Find something in your classroom that is approximately that height from the floor. Measure and write its actual height.
   (c) If the record for the high jump doubled in the 2012 Olympics, how high would that be? Do you think that is possible? Give your reasons.

133

Weight

Let's investigate

Mamma Pat made a big bowl of pasta.

Papa Pat took some first.

Then Mamma Pat took hers.

Joey Pat had some.

Sophie Pat had some too.

Little Marco had what was left. He had 150 g of pasta.

Each took half the amount of the person before.

How much pasta did Mamma Pat make?

1. Convert these lengths into the unit of measure given.
   - (a) 2000 g = _____ kg
   - (b) 5000 g = _____ kg
   - (c) 9000 g = _____ kg
   - (d) 5040 g = _____ kg and _____ g
   - (e) 500 g = _____ kg
   - (f) 1000 g = _____ kg
   - (g) 4080 g = _____ kg and _____ g
   - (h) 1.5 kg = _____ g
   - (i) 3.5 kg = _____ g
   - (j) 1 kg = _____ g
   - (k) 2 kg = _____ g
   - (l) 8.50 kg = _____ g
   - (m) 0.5 kg = _____ g
   - (n) 10 kg = _____ g

2 A baker has a big order of cakes he needs to bake.

He needs five oranges for his recipe.

Each orange weighs 150 g.

What is the total weight of the oranges?
- (a) In grams?
- (b) In kilograms?

3 A gardener has 20 plants to pot.

Each plant pot needs 50 g of soil.

How much soil does the gardener need altogether?
- (a) In grams?
- (b) In kilograms and grams?

4 A builder has to fix four walls that have fallen down.

He needs 3 kg of cement for each wall.

How much cement will he need altogether?
- (a) In kilograms?
- (b) In grams?

5 In the kitchen was a large piece of cheese. It weighed 1200 g.

A mouse ate half of it before another mouse came.

They ate half of what was left equally between them before another mouse came.

All three mice then finished the cheese.
They ate equal amounts.

How much cheese did each mouse eat?

Weight (2)

Let's investigate

Which weighs more, a kilogram of pebbles or a kilogram of feathers?

Explain your reasoning.

1. You want to have a party for 20 people, but you have to change some recipes ready for more guests.

   Copy and complete these recipes.

   (a)

Ingredients for Shortbread
Makes 10 biscuits
240 g flour
180 g fat
100 g sugar

   To make 20 biscuits

   Double the quantity of the ingredients for shortbread and write the amount in grams

   _____ g flour
   _____ g fat
   _____ g sugar

   (b)

Ingredients for fruit biscuits
Makes 5 biscuits
125 g flour
50 g fat
75 g sugar
30 g fruit

   To make 20 biscuits

   Quadruple (multiply by 4) the quantity of the ingredients for fruit biscuits and write the amount in grams

   _____ g flour
   _____ g fat
   _____ g sugar
   _____ g fruit

(c)
Ingredients for pasta sauce

Makes enough for 3

380 g tomatoes

130 g onions

70 g carrots

30 g cheese

To make enough for 30

Multiply by 10 the quantity of the ingredients for pasta sauce and write the amount in kilograms and grams

_____ kg _____ g tomatoes

_____ kg _____ g onions

_____ kg _____ g carrots

_____ kg _____ g cheese

2 Copy and complete this table

kilograms (kg)	kg and g	grams (g)
1.25 kg	1 kg 250 g	1250 g
1.5 kg		
	1 kg 900 g	
0.7 kg		
	1 kg 750 g	
0.24 kg		
		380 g
		2040 g

3 You have a balance scale with four weights. With these four weights you can balance any whole number load (in grams) from 1 to 40.

How much should each of the four weights be? (You can place weights on both sides of the scale at the same time)

4 Professor Potts needs to find the weight of each test tube for his experiments.

He had three colours:

The professor knows that when green and red are on the scales together they weight 440 grams.

When green and yellow are on the scales together they weigh 320 grams.

When yellow and red are on the scales together they weigh 180 grams.

How much does each colour tube weigh?